The NCTE High School L

The NCTE High School Literature Series offers classroom teachers in-depth studies of individual writers. Grounded in theory, each volume focuses on a single author and features excerpts from the writer's works, biographical information, and samples of professional literary criticism. Rich in opportunities for classroom discussion and writing assignments that teachers can adapt to their own literature curriculum, each book also offers many examples of student writing.

Volumes in the Series

Langston Hughes in the Classroom

"Do Nothin' till You Hear from Me"

The NCTE High School Literature Series

Carmaletta M. Williams

Johnson County Community College, Overland Park, Kansas

NATIONAL COUNCIL OF TEACHERS OF ENGLISH
1111 W. KENYON ROAD, URBANA, ILLINOIS 61801-1096

Poetry reprinted from THE COLLECTED POEMS OF LANGSTON HUGHES by Langston Hughes, copyright © 1994 by The Estate of Langston Hughes. Used by permission of Alfred A. Knopf, a division of Random House, Inc.

Cover photo provided by Van Vechten Trust and Yale Collection of American Literature, Beinecke Rare Book and Manuscript Library.

Staff Editor: Bonny Graham
Interior Design: Jenny Jensen Greenleaf
Cover Design: Jenny Jensen Greenleaf and Tom Jaczak

NCTE Stock Number: 25611

©2006 by the National Council of Teachers of English.

It is the policy of NCTE in its journals and other publications to provide a forum for the open discussion of ideas concerning the content and the teaching of English and the language arts. Publicity accorded to any particular point of view does not imply endorsement by the Executive Committee, the Board of Directors, or the membership at large, except in announcements of policy, where such endorsement is clearly specified.

Every effort has been made to provide current URLs and e-mail addresses, but because of the rapidly changing nature of the Web, some sites and addresses may no longer be accessible.

Library of Congress Cataloging-in-Publication Data
Williams, Carmaletta M.
    Langston Hughes in the classroom : "do nothin' till you hear from me" / Carmaletta M. Williams.
        p. cm. — (The NCTE high school literature series)
    Includes bibliographical references.
    ISBN 0-8141-2561-1 (pbk.)
    1. Hughes, Langston, 1902–1967—Study and teaching (Secondary)
2. African Americans in literature—Study and teaching (Secondary) I. Title.
II. Series.
    PS3515.U274Z95 2006
    818' .5209—dc22

                                                                    2006002426

For my mothers who bought me books,
Taught me to read,
And instilled a love of learning
Doris Rebecca Grant
And
The Late Blanche Waters Blue

Contents

Acknowledgments

Nothing wonderful happens in isolation. That is certainly true of this study guide to teaching the works of Langston Hughes. This is my heartfelt acknowledgment of the incredible people who supported me during this endeavor. First is my mother, Doris Rebecca Grant. She sacrificed precious time that we could have spent together and encouraged me to "keep working." My sister and her husband, Mitchi and Melvin Payne, and their daughter, Morgan, have been accommodating in relieving me of some familial responsibilities. My sons, Jason, Chief, and Nick, were abundantly patient and kept me entertained. My (grand)daughter, who during the writing of this guide changed her name to Antoinette Jacine Maria Williams to incorporate my middle name, Maria, into hers, probably made the biggest sacrifice in terms of losing my time. Olivia, Jason II, and J. Ivan's "I love you, too, Grandma" kept me going. Many thanks also to Aunt Vickie, who kept us nourished. I thank Dr. Maryemma Graham, who rescued me in my time of need and also told me about this project. She has been a rock. University of Kansas Chancellor Robert Hemenway has provided invaluable support. Dr. John Thomson, my academic dean, has been patient with the challenge that working with me provides. I also want to thank my teacher-friends who reviewed and commented on the manuscript: Quintonella Bennett, Tony Harris, Treina Raines, and Brittney Turner. Last, and certainly not least, Dr. John Edgar Tidwell has been an incredible support to me during this and other projects. I thank you from the bottom of my heart. NCTE's Dr. Zarina Hock is in a category of her own. Her vision and focus for this literature series are remarkable. She is truly determined to better high school literature teachers' lives, lighten their loads, and make teaching literature easier.

Introduction

The rich melody and poignant lyrics of Langston Hughes's (1902–1967) favorite song, "Do Nothin' till You Hear from Me," are symbolic of the richly woven tapestries of art that generations of Hughes lovers have come to appreciate in his work. The marvelous pictures of poets Maya Angelou and Amiri Baraka dancing at the Schomburg Center for Research in Black Culture at the New York Public Library to that song as Hughes's ashes were scattered are the perfect symbolic tribute to the man who loved words and books, loved music, loved Harlem, and most of all loved people, especially Black people. Thus, I thought it absolutely appropriate to name this book that guides teachers through the study of the life and work of Langston Hughes after that song.

This guide is structured to make it as easy as possible for high school teachers to learn about Hughes and to teach Hughes. I truly believe that this guide is serviceable for both you and your students. When I wrote this book, I envisioned high school junior and senior classrooms and some accelerated first-year–sophomore classes getting excited as they learned about Langston Hughes. My experience working with high school teachers has been that they often feel overwhelmed when trying to introduce material with which they are unfamiliar. Sad as it is to say, as important an author as Hughes is, his work has not always been included in mainstream curricula. The teachers often confess to missing subtle points in the reading, which is easy to do as Hughes contextualizes his works in time and with social and political events. That is the reason I included the elements that may read a bit like plot summaries. I give you full credit for being able to read and understand the stories, so, of course, I am not summarizing the plot for you. What I am trying to do is be careful to help you understand the material and the points that Hughes was making. There is a rich vein of Americana in the works of Hughes that you and your students can tap into easily with just a little extra insight, which I provide here.

My primary intent was to construct each unit so that it can be used independently of the others. There are, however, some inter-sections in the text. Because Hughes's life experiences are such an integral part of his work, the first sections demonstrate how Hughes's life and art coalesce. Of course, in a guide such as this, we cannot address all such cases, so the other units are divided into significant genres of his work. Hughes was one of the few writers of the Harlem Renaissance who was able to support himself with his writing. He wrote prolifically: poetry, novels, short stories, plays, librettos, po-litical propaganda, and autobiography. For the high school teacher, the more significant genres are autobiography, poetry, and the novel; therefore, they are the focus of this text.

Chapter 3 discusses the role of the era in Hughes's work because it is also essential that you have a good understanding of the New Negro Movement and the Harlem Renaissance. Hughes's work is certainly influenced by that era. Many of the images and responses in his work are framed by the sociocultural events of the era. This exciting era was vibrant with cultural ferment and possibly was the most transformative time for African American arts and letters.

Also, where it is important to know, I talk about critical responses to Hughes. I do not devote a separate section to criticism on Hughes but instead mention the critics in individual chapters in order to contextualize the information. Hughes's work is experiencing an incredible resurgence in scholarship. There is an abundance of literary criticism on his work, with more coming out each day, mostly because he was prolific and is still considered extremely important in the history of American literature. The University of Missouri Press has and is continuing to publish multivolume collections of his work, each volume edited by an eminent Hughes scholar. The introductions to the collections are themselves insightful reads.

The second part of each chapter is the In the Classroom section. Here I have created teaching modules that draw parallels and connect the people, places, and events in Hughes's work to your students' lives. In these sections, I include uncorrected samples of my students' work. Experiencing Hughes's work is much more exciting for your students when they see him as an artist who speaks to current cultural events and not just as "some old guy" who wrote in the 1930s and 1940s, long before even their parents were born. (Although this is not always an assumption we should feel free to make. I had a student recently who told me that her father was born in 1928. Her mother, she volunteered, was much younger.)

I have contextualized Hughes's life and work in the chronology, where I have attempted to include the major social and political events that had a significant impact on his life and appear, in some form or another, in his work. I have also included personal information about him and his family as well as a listing of his professional work.

In the selected bibliography, I have chosen those works that I think will be most beneficial for an understanding of Hughes. I include those sources I find most important because of the content, the scholar who wrote the piece, or its potential use for you as a classroom teacher. The same holds true for the very limited listing of Web sites and films. My hope is that these readings stimulate you to further reading.

A glossary of significant terms appears at the end of this book. As teachers, you have knowledge of the genre and of the vocabulary. The list is included as a guide to language that your students should learn. So if it seems that some of the terms are too basic, remember that I am reminding you of terminology your students need to know.

I want to point out what may appear as an inconsistency in the text. To maintain the language of Hughes and his generation, in some parts of this text I refer to African Americans as "Negroes" or "Coloreds." Even though current vernacular refers to *People of Color*, that term should not be confused with *colored people*. They are two entirely different references. You should make it clear to your students that those identifiers used in the text and in the criticism, and which will certainly surface in their discussions, such as "Negro," "colored," and even "nigger," are completely inappropriate except for discussions such as this one, which are set for the most part in a particular time. When necessary to retain the integrity of the piece, I engage the language of Hughes and his contemporaries. Otherwise, I use the terms *African American* or *Black*, as should you and your students.

It is important that we study and teach Hughes because he is arguably one of the most significant American poets. Notice this came without the qualifier "African American." His works have survived and thrived in the turbulent, transformative decades since he wrote them. Politicians quote him, artists model their work after his, students embrace him, and those of us whose souls need poetry love him. I have attempted to make this study guide user-friendly, or "teacher-friendly." I certainly appreciate and share the complications that come with having to teach too much material in too short a time frame. It was my goal to have each chapter "turnkey," in that you can choose whichever one suits your curriculum and have that chapter provide useful background information about Hughes, the genre, and teaching modules that you can take directly into your classroom without much extra work.

Happy reading! I hope you and your students appreciate the life and works of Langston Hughes as much as I do.

1 Learning about Langston

Students sometimes feel that successful people have led wonderful, stress-free lives. As high school teachers, you can use Hughes's life as a model of transformation and triumph. Next to Maya Angelou, who probably holds the record of any literary figure for reinventing herself the most times, Hughes constantly crafted the life he wanted for himself at the time he wanted it. When he needed the sea, he became a seaman and sailed the world. When he needed to speak out against social and political injustices, he attended John Reed Club meetings and wrote political propaganda for them. When he needed art, he became a writer and lived and wrote alongside other artists and intellectuals, the Talented Tenth of the Harlem Renaissance. When Hughes needed to be in the performance arts and around performers, he wrote plays and librettos and produced and directed them. When he needed to be a part of the folk, he hung around the barbershop, in revolutionary Black Arts poet Amiri Baraka's apartment, and at pool halls, bars, and literary salons. Hughes took control of his life and how he wanted to live it. Teach that possibility to your students. They can craft, form, and reform their lives as they wish, when they wish, as many times as they wish. Teach them, through Hughes, to believe in themselves and their endless possibilities.

Through his remarkable life's journey, Hughes gave us a storehouse of materials and teaching tools. As high school teachers, you have a marvelous opportunity to make a poet real to your students. You can collapse time to bring a decades-old era to the present. You can also use his work to validate the lives of your students, many of whom, like Hughes, have traveled troubled roads.

Life was not always fine for James Langston Hughes. Just as he wrote about in his poem "Life Is Fine," his life was in constant flux and filled with contradiction. In fact, it is not even clear when he lost the first name he shared with his father or if anyone in his family ever called him "James." We do know that when Hughes testified before Senator Joseph McCarthy and the House Un-American Activities Committee in 1953, he identified himself as "James Langston Hughes" and said that when he wrote he used only "Langston Hughes," but that his friends knew all his names. If they knew them, they did not use them. None of the literary people who identified themselves as his friends and wrote about Hughes ever referred to him as "James" in their works, so the identification of those friends is a bit muddled. What is clear is that the world came to know the work and love the man they called by his middle name.

Langston Hughes was born on a troubled road. In 1899, his father, James Nathaniel Hughes, upset and angry with the Oklahoma Territory's all-White examining board for not allowing him to take the bar exam after he had studied law by correspondence, took his wife and moved to Joplin, Missouri. On February 1, 1902, Langston was born. His father could not cope with the pressures of trying to raise a child and taking care of a wife in abject poverty, especially under the social, economic, and professional constraints of being African American in early twentieth century America. When Langston was eighteen months old, his father left. He left Langston, his wife, and his country. James Hughes moved to Cuba, and then to Mexico.

Langston Hughes's mother, Carolina "Carrie" Langston Hughes, refused to go with her husband. This imposed a terrible financial hardship, as Carrie was unable to find meaningful work in Joplin. So she moved from town to town with baby Langston in tow. When the responsibility of taking care of him and trying to work a series of low-paying jobs became too much for her, she took Langston to Lawrence, Kansas, to live with her mother. Over the next twelve years, the young Langston would sometimes, but not often, live with Carrie. He started school in Topeka, Kansas, where Carrie, who had attended the University of Kansas for a while, worked as a "stenographer for a colored lawyer . . . named Mr. Guy" (Hughes, *Big Sea* 14).

In Topeka, Carrie introduced her son to the theater, to libraries, and to books. She also insisted that Langston attend Harrison Street School, the White school a few blocks from the rented room they shared. There, Langston learned many lessons. He learned that his mother was a fighter and had not hesitated to go before the school board to insist that her son be admitted to that school. He learned that most of the White teachers he would interact with were kind and thoughtful, but he also learned that some were not. One teacher's racist remarks prompted some of the White children to grab weapons, in the form of stones and tin cans, out of an alley and chase Langston home. This incident also taught him not to hate all White people: some of his young classmates came to his rescue and saved him from the bullies.

When Langston was about five or six years old, Carrie and her estranged husband decided to reconcile. She took her son and her mother with her to Mexico in anticipation of that reunion.

The first night they were in Mexico an earthquake forced tarantulas out of the walls, drove people from their homes and theaters into the alameda, and scared Carrie back to Kansas. She and her husband were never to reconcile.

Carrie continued to move from town to town in search of a better job and a better life. When the opportunity presented itself, she took her son with her. But their times together were brief and sporadic. Most of the first thirteen years of Langston's life were spent in abject poverty living with his maternal grandmother in Lawrence.

Langston's young life followed the flow first established by his mother, father, and grandmother. His soul, however, like the soul he writes about in the poem "The Negro Speaks of Rivers," sought solace in the depths of his racial heritage. It was somewhat harder for him to come to terms with his personal heritage.

Langston's father became relatively successful in Mexico after a time and began to contribute minimally to Langston's needs. Carrie continued her sporadic involvement in his life, and his functional relatives, Auntie and Uncle Reed, were his caretakers for a short while after his grandmother died. With all of these influences, it needs to be clarified that Langston's primary path in life was laid by his grandmother, Mary Leary Langston. She generated an aura of racial and personal esteem. The racial pride she taught him is evident in all of Hughes's work. Hughes, for example, recounts his pride in her on an occasion when, as the last surviving widow of John Brown's raid on Harper's Ferry, she traveled with him to Osawatomie, Kansas, where President Teddy Roosevelt spoke. Young Langston was proud and impressed to see his grandmother sitting on the platform with the president while he made a speech honoring her. Mrs. Langston's first husband, a freedman, had fought alongside John Brown at Harper's Ferry in 1859 and was killed in that raid on the federal arsenal.

Her second husband, Charles Langston, searching for greater racial and financial freedom, moved to Kansas. His deep desire for autonomy and the ability to progress beyond the strictures he found in farm life enticed him to own a store in Lawrence. He paid little attention to his business, however, and consequently died penniless. He left little more than memories of his quest to fulfill those desires for equity in America and a talent for literary expression that he passed on to his grandson.

But Hughes doesn't end his description of his grandparents by focusing on their disappointments and poverty. He tells us that his grandfather was not the only family member with writing talent or political acumen. In 1894, Charles's brother, John Mercer Langston, who shared his energy and enthusiasm for freedom fighting, wrote his autobiography, *From the Virginia Plantation to the National Capital* [sic] (*Big Sea* 13). In 1855, John Mercer Langston was perhaps the first Black American to be elected to public office when he became town clerk in Brownhelm, Ohio. Both brothers knew the importance of money and had a commitment to political service. When John Mercer Langston died, he left his heirs stocks, bonds, and a large house. Charles Langston, however, left his wife memories, "some fine speeches," and a home she had to mortgage in order to take care of herself and young Langston. But this is not a tragic ending; Hughes makes it clear that more important than money was the inspiring legacy of the fight for freedom that Mrs. Langston and her husbands shared and passed on to their progeny.

Like the family in Hughes's poem "Mother to Son," life for Langston was no crystal stair.

Mother to Son
Langston Hughes

Well, son, I'll tell you:
Life for me ain't been no crystal stair.
It's had tacks in it.
And splinters,
And boards torn up.
And places with no carpet on the floor—
Bare.
But all the time
I'se been a-climbin-on,
And reachin' landin's,
And turnin' corners,
And sometimes goin' in the dark
Where there ain't been no light.
So boy, don't you turn back.
Don't you set down on the steps
'Cause you finds it's kinder hard.
Don't you fall now—
For I'se still goin', honey.
I'se still climbin'
And life for me ain't been no crystal stair.

While the young Langston lived in Lawrence, his life was filled with music, poetry, and books, but also with an abbreviated family, poverty, and loneliness. Mary Leary Langston, part Native American and part African American, was a proud and gentle woman. Unlike many other women in her financial position, Mary Langston did not do domestic work. She became a landlord instead. She rented out rooms in her house to students at the University of Kansas. If she could rent out the whole house, Mrs. Langston and her grandson would sometimes move in with close family friends James and Mary Reed. The ten to twelve dollars a month she would net from her rents was not enough money to lift them out of poverty or even enough to provide basic necessities for her and Langston, but it did pay the mortgage. (Sadly, shortly after her death, the house reverted to the mortgage company.)

Life was not always easy for Langston and his grandmother, but they had each other for emotional support. They found spiritual enrichment and comfort at St. Luke African Methodist Episcopal (A.M.E.) Church. In addition to supplementing the Christian education encouraged by his grandmother and promoted by Auntie Reed ("Uncle Reed was a sinner and never went to church as long as he lived, nor cared anything about it. . . . But both of them were good and kind—the one who went to church and the one who didn't. And no doubt from them I learned to like both Christians and sinners equally well" [Hughes, *Big Sea* 18]), the church was a source of many of the rhythms Langston credits as being an influence on his poetry.

Hughes confesses, however, in his autobiography *The Big Sea* that in his youth he wasn't always eager to attend services. He reflects on the lingering emotional pain and personal embarrassment he suffered for once faking a religious conversion. The pain of harboring the lie that he had seen Jesus and deceiving Auntie Reed and the rest of the parishioners one night at St. Luke into thinking he had experienced a conversion caused Langston not to believe in Jesus because "he didn't come to help" (*Big Sea* 21). Langston realized that by faking a vision he had trespassed on the faith that Auntie Reed had in him. As far as we know, neither the Reeds nor the parishioners ever learned of his deceit. This "falling out" with Jesus lasted throughout Hughes's life and surfaced repeatedly in his political poems. In fact, one of his most radical pieces, the poem "Goodbye Christ," created such an unfavorable response from the public that Hughes had to repudiate the poem and apologize. Hughes biographer Arnold Rampersad, in his introduction to *The Collected Poems of Langston Hughes*, says that "Hughes . . . wrote some of the most radical poems ever published by an American, as well as some of the most poignant lamentations of the chasm that often exists between American social ideals and American social reality" (4).

Mary Leary Langston believed so much in the potential of her grandson to succeed against the odds he was facing in the United States that not only did she insist that he attend church and Sunday school, but she and the Reeds were also adamant that he get a good education, which she considered the key to unlocking his future. After attending first grade in Topeka, Kansas, where his mother was then working, Langston entered Pinckney School in Lawrence for the second grade. At Pinckney, Langston, along with all the other primary-level African American children, was taught in a separate room by an African American teacher. The segregation did not affect his ability or eagerness to learn. His love of books, which had its nascence in 1907 when his mother took him with her to "the little vine-covered library on the grounds of the capitol in Topeka" (*Big Sea* 26), continued to grow. At that library, he fell in love with librarians and with libraries. Then when he was six, "books began to happen" to him, so much so that he "believed in books more than people" (16). Books were constant, unwavering, and good company. Langston's love and belief in books charted the exciting artistic, social, and political paths his life would follow.

During the time Langston lived with the Reeds, he attended New York School. Bright and precocious, Langston often disrupted his fourth-grade classroom and aggravated his teacher with unsolicited comments. By the time he entered the eighth grade, he was living in Cleveland with his mother and stepfather, Homer

Clark, and his little stepbrother Gwyn, nicknamed Kit. Langston's teacher at Central School, Ida Lyons, moved all the African American children into what Langston called "the Jim Crow row." Protesting the segregation, Langston and some of his friends were remanded to the principal's office. Not placidly accepting overt racism was probably an inherent reaction in him. Langston's grandmother had espoused the belief that all people should be free and passed it on to her daughter and her grandson. That may have been one of the reasons Carrie was attracted to a man like James Nathaniel Hughes, who left the country rather than live under the constraints of racism. Likewise, when Langston convinced his friends that there was something wrong with being relegated to the Jim Crow row and protested it, his resistance was perfectly natural. The young revolutionaries were expelled from the school for their efforts. The children were reinstated, however, when a prominent physician, Dr. Grant Harvey, intervened on their behalf.

Langston's quest for an education was not a smooth, straight road in Kansas, Ohio, New York, or Pennsylvania. Getting an education in Lawrence, Kansas, especially wasn't easy, but it was effective. Langston received a sound educational foundation in Lawrence schools and libraries. He also often spent Saturday afternoons at University of Kansas sporting events, particularly football games, rooting for the Jayhawks, shouting for them to "walk chalk." I don't know whether the grown-up Hughes misremembered the real chant, which is "rock chalk," or whether Langston as a child actually thought the words were "walk chalk." In truth, it doesn't matter. What is important is that he had fun in the crowd rooting for the football team, captured a warm childhood memory, and learned how to entertain himself by becoming part of a community.

IN THE CLASSROOM:
Community Commemorations

Even more important than Hughes remembering Lawrence, Kansas, is that Lawrence remembers Langston Hughes. Those facilities he frequented as a child and the town that provided a home for him came to recognize the contributions that Hughes had made to them and to the world. The new Pinckney School, which was built in 1930 and sits further back on the same lot as the old one, in 1991 named its library The Langston Hughes Library for Children. A movement is underway to rename the old Carnegie Public Library after Hughes. The Lawrence City Hall bears prophetic words from Hughes's poem "Youth" on its façade: "We have tomorrow bright before us like a flame." The places and the homes he shared with his grandmother and with the Reeds have either been transformed or disappeared, but their influence on Hughes's life and the lessons he learned in Lawrence live on in his work. Teach that possibility to your students.

As a teacher, you will find that a unit on Langston Hughes gives you an opportunity to create a research project that connects your students to the history of their community. Cultural memory was extremely important to Hughes, as it should be to all of us. Knowing who Phillis Wheatley was and why the school is named after her enriches the learning experience of the students who attend that school. Reading the poetry of Phillis Wheatley makes her even more real. Educator and writer Doug Hunt argues that the knowledge that matters, at least in English classes, is moral knowledge or uplifting knowledge. Read his *Misunderstanding the Assignment* for a complete discussion of why students need to know the moral and historical development of their communities. Studying community commemorations also helps students get past the dualism inherent in earlier instruction that taught them to look for what is either right or wrong in a text. Hunt also encourages us to move our students past multi-pluralism, or what he has identified as the "whatever" attitude: the attitude that everybody has a right to her or his opinion, so whatever I write is fine.

Finding a middle ground between rigid hierarchies of right and wrong and an "anything goes" attitude is important when we consider the works of important writers. For example, the John Reed Clubs were socialist, which does not mean that Hughes was not doing important, valuable, moral work in the literary field when he wrote for them. The same goes for other people com-memorated in your students' communities. People who are some-times outside the norms of acceptable behaviors can do worthwhile work for a community. During the Harlem Renaissance, for ex-ample, Casper Holstein, who I have termed a "benevolent gang-ster," contributed the money that funded many literary contests for young people.

On the other hand, some communities downplay the histo-ries that are embarrassing, hurtful, or disparaging of the lives of some of the people in those communities. Your students should develop an awareness of the difference between commemorating a positive influence in the community and "shoving it in the face" of other members of the community. Just look at the hurt feelings and anger that surface when the Confederate flag is flown in cer-tain communities. For some people, the flag represents the sacri-fices of forefathers. For others, it represents the racism their fore-fathers endured. In a public lecture, filmmaker Kevin Willmott argued that the Confederate flag should be confined to a museum and never allowed to fly because of the hurt feelings it promotes.

Let your students study issues, take a stand, and justify their choices.

Every community has facilities named after prominent persons. The assignment for your students is to understand why. In better understanding the relationship between those persons and students' lives, students increase their ability to gain insight into historical and literary allusions. Depending on the size of your community, you can assign or have students choose different sites to research the history of the person after whom the building, park, street, etc., was named. Their research might include going to the site, especially if it is one in which the person actually lived, ate, or visited, and walking around it or around part of it if it isn't possible, safe, or legal to walk the entire grounds. Students can be looking for historical markers, monuments, or other tributes to the person for whom it was named. They should also be trying to feel some of the person's spirit there.

A good way to frame this assignment is as either an observation paper or a biography of the person connected to the monumental tribute. Having students research the political processes and documents, such as city council meeting minutes, involved in the naming of the place is a good way to get them deeply involved in the project. I have found it best to avoid having my students write testimonials of the person. They all read like obituaries, which gets pretty depressing after about the twentieth one. I have also come to recognize that my students skip the "hard facts" when they write testimonials. I don't select the places for them, but I encourage them to avoid controversial places that might lead to arguments on "hot topics" like women's centers, which tend to digress into abortion rights debates. Instead, this assignment requires students to adapt a perspective and develop a method of investigation that allows them to learn about the person, situate him or her historically, and understand the moral and historical imperatives that led to the commemoration.

Students comment in their reports on whether the building reflects the person's life, interests, and work. For example, green was Langston Hughes's favorite color. He wrote almost everything in green ink. Any building that is supposed to serve as a tribute to him should have green included in its color scheme, if nothing other than a broad green stripe on the wall. If the person after whom the building was named had a special interest in the artwork of children or of nature, then your students might note whether there is any juvenile or natural art in the building. If your students go to the Magic Johnson Theatres in Los Angeles, they will surely note the basketball memorabilia included in the facility. The point is to have students recognize the difference between slapping someone's name on a marker and creating a genuine tribute to that person's life, work, and legacy.

This assignment can be further expanded by having your students write to the managers of the facility, either to congratulate them on the marvelous job done in reflecting the life and work of the designee or to make suggestions to improve the tribute.

The Freedom Tree

Another assignment my students enjoy is the "Freedom Tree." This exercise lets them connect history with the works of Langston Hughes. The project gives them experience in researching local history, interviewing local individuals, and writing short, concise statements. Hughes is a good model for this project because information about his life and community is readily available, and most of it can be reduced to sound-bite-size statements that fit perfectly on a leaf of the trees they create, whether on paper or in electronic format. I teach in Kansas, which claims Hughes as a favorite son, so this is an especially interesting project for my students. This assignment is easily adapted to other writers.

Langston Hughes was especially interested in establishing human rights and social equity for all. As a socialist thinker, though he denied being a member of the Communist Party, he was especially concerned with class distinctions. He wanted all persons to have equal protection and access in this country. Creating the Freedom Tree allows our students to see that none of the results of civil rights legislation came about on their own. For early European Americans, the quest for freedom was rooted in the events that culminated in the American Revolution. For First Americans —Native Americans—the struggle began when "others" invaded their lands. For African Americans, the struggle began when the first foot was forced onto a slave ship in Africa; their Freedom Tree was planted in 1619, or even a century earlier, when the first Africans were brought to the Americas. Slave narratives and other historical documents reveal that never did those people lose their desire or stop their fight for freedom. Your students' research will reveal that this is true for the people of other designations. For Langston Hughes and other members of the Talented Tenth of the Harlem Renaissance, freedom came with the ability to express themselves in their own ways.

I don't have a classroom that only I use, so my students create a virtual tree on PowerPoint. Although this is fun, I would prefer to have them build a paper Freedom Tree. The form and size of the tree, of course, will be restricted by space, but allow students to decide how their tree will look. Because a tree grows over time from the ground upwards, the students should be careful to put information in chronological order. The labels should explain the significance of the event. Instead of simply adding a leaf that says, for example, "*Brown v. Board of Education of Topeka, KS*, May 17,

1954, Supreme Court decision," the students need to mention that this decision overturned the legal segregation that had been established in 1896 with the *Plessy v. Ferguson* Supreme Court decision and that it was the law for desegregating public schools. Pictures, drawings, photographs, and graphs can and should be included on the tree. The tree should be historically accurate, visually aesthetic, have grammatically correct "leaves," and, most of all, reflect the creativity of the students. My students even have squirrels pop up on our PowerPoint trees when something exciting happened.

W. E. B. DuBois says that "the root of the trees rather than the leaves is the source of its life" (87). Because I like for my students to see the work of writers in context, first they map out the roots of the Tree of Freedom of the United States, then of Hughes's life, and then sometimes of their particular communities.

Artistically and politically, Hughes's life exemplifies this immersion in the freedom struggle. Encourage students to look at his life in the context of freedom. They will discover that Hughes came from a family of freedom fighters. His family tree parallels the Freedom Tree of the State of Kansas. Even though the state was originally established as a Free State in order to keep out Blacks, this designation did not stop the massive migration of African Americans into Kansas. Every community has its own history and literatures of freedom. This information is readily available in local libraries and historical societies. Much of it is available online.

This assignment serves well as a device for teaching our students to contextualize literature. We need to teach them that the conflicts, characters, and settings in every piece of literature they read are contextualized historically. Time and place function to create conflict. For example, the reason the narrator succumbs to madness in Charlotte Perkins Gilman's "The Yellow Wallpaper" is complicated by the time setting. We now understand postpartum depression, which was completely unrecognized during the time in which the story was set. In Hughes's "Cora Unashamed," the protagonist's problems are rooted in her isolation within a community that includes no people who share her racial and cultural identity.

When your students create a Freedom Tree, they should be careful to examine the roots to be sure they have grounded the tree in good historical and literary soil. Some of the information they should be looking for is the evolution of the freedom movement in their own communities:

- Where and when it started.

- Is the movement still active, or do the people who were involved consider it a fait accompli?

- The names of some of the people who are or were critical in the movement—more than the media faces, students should be concerned with the grassroots folk who were little recognized, the people who worked behind the scenes.

- The names of the people who wrote the literature of the effort. Recent "WalMart wars," for example, have instigated a wealth of writing by community activists.

- The people who are vital to maintaining the movement or, as Rev. Jesse Jackson says, the ones who keep hope alive.

- Where help in achieving goals came from, such as the Justice Department or the president of the United States or the mayor.

- The catalysts for justice, such as television during the modern civil rights movement of the 1950s and 1960s, which helped stir public opinion with broadcasts of the scenes of injustices, such as fire hoses and dogs being turned on children.

- Some of the pitfalls and downfalls, such as loss of jobs, burned out houses, and death.

- Laws and legislation that were a result of the movement, such as the Civil Rights Act of 1964, the Voting Rights Act of 1965, and public accommodations laws, or local zoning laws.

- Court decisions that were important to achieving goals, like *Brown v. Board of Education of Topeka, Kansas*.

- The sacrifices in lives, money, social position, etc., that were made to achieve the goals of the movement.

Students are often surprised to learn that their parents and grand-parents are rich sources for this project. One of my students learned that her grandmother had made picket signs for a strike at her job; another found that hers had walked across the Edmund Pettus Bridge in Selma, Alabama.

Because this is an English class, it's important to have students look for significant writers of the time or works that focus on that time. Including on the tree the works of writers that students have already read makes this very easy and also a richer learning experience. Students rethink certain conflicts and incidents in the works and cross-reference them with the sociopolitical events of the times. The tricky part of this research is to make sure students are identifying the time as it is depicted in the work, not the date the work was written or published. A contemporary author writing a historical novel will be focused on the social mores of the time of the story, not those of the twenty-first century.

As a guide to understanding the tree, students can collect their sources and create a bibliography. Even though encyclopedias can be encouraged as a beginning point, I like for my students to look beyond them for information. Reading old newspaper articles is informative and also a good exercise; it sends students to the library where they can smell the books. (A friend of mine at the University of Kansas said he had a student who confessed that he had almost graduated without going to the library. That would have been a tragedy.) My students also like to look at historically accurate (as far as creative nonfiction allows) movies, videos, and documentaries. Encourage students to interview relatives and friends; as one of my students admitted, he "just talked with the old people down the block. They were so old they had to know *something*." Encourage your students to consult both print and nonprint sources, but limit the number of Internet sources because these can create too many distractions. Besides, my experience has been that students aren't careful to check the validity of the Internet sources they download. They need to learn to critically examine their sources to avoid including worthless information.

2 Migration, Mobility, and the Folk: Where Life and Art Intersect

In giving himself the richly deserved title of "folk poet" (Rampersad, *Collected Poems* 4), Hughes established the tone and mission of all his writing: he was the voice of the common people, the persons whom Hughes referred to as "the folk." To Hughes the folk were a beautiful mosaic of American culture. They were all those people caught in voiceless, powerless positions who found themselves divorced from and desiring the American dream. The folk were also those people of all colors and political ideologies who were struggling to end classism and racism in this country, especially for themselves and their children. "The people" were those very rich, privileged persons who indulged in the luxury of the American dream, oblivious to the conditions of the American underclass.

Even though Hughes himself moved easily through a multicultural world and wrote for and about all who populated it, foremost the folk that Hughes wrote about were African Americans, especially those migrants who found themselves displaced in the urban North. These are the people that Hughes in his essay "The Negro Artist and the Racial Mountain" describes as having a "nip of gin" on Saturday nights, and who don't see themselves as too important, too well-fed, or too learned to participate in life. When they are happy, they're ecstatic; when they are moved spiritually, they shout; and all the time they remain true to themselves in the midst of a culture that demands conformity.

The value in recognizing and appreciating the life of the migrants in Hughes's work is that it allows our students to feel the immediacy of these people's lives. In the classroom, you need to connect the relevance of the population mobility of the first half of the twentieth century that Hughes writes about to our constantly on-the-move twenty-first century culture. Sandy in Hughes's novel *Not without Laughter* moves constantly because of his parents' instability. Harriett in the same novel is chronically mobile because she is trying to achieve fame as a blues singer. The Dark Girl in the poem of the same name is emotionally lost in the North after moving to find a better life. Jesse B. Semple in Hughes's Simple stories moves to find a job in a factory.

The journeys of these people, as well as their arrivals at their destinations and attempts to survive in the foreignness of the urban South or the industrialized North, especially in Harlem, are dominant themes in Hughes's work. Movement, travel, and feeling displaced are constant themes in his work. Journeys also symbolize Hughes's own life, as well as the lives of the people of whom he writes. Just like the narrator in his poem "Dream Variations," Hughes flung his arms wide, found his place in the sun, and danced, whirled, and wrote his way through a marvelous yet sometimes troubled life.

Born in Joplin, Missouri, raised in Lawrence, Kansas, and graduated high school in Cleveland, Ohio, Hughes also traveled the oceans working on freighter ships and lived and wrote in Africa, Europe (especially Russia), Asia, and other parts of the world. These journeys provided the experiences that molded into manhood the child born in the midst of his father's disappointment with the United States and raised in his mother's instability; they then carried him to the places and people that nourished and nurtured his creativity. Through all these travels, Hughes rooted his soul in Harlem, New York. Hughes embraced his failures and his losses as well as his successes. He enjoyed life in the United States and his struggle not to be consumed by a land that in his time often vilified Blacks yet saw them as exotic "others."

More than a superficial understanding of Hughes's art cannot be achieved without an exploration of the importance of movement in his life. In teaching Hughes, impress on your students that here was a man who traveled the world sharing his art with people of all cultures. Hughes blossomed and thrived through his travels. Yet a close examination of his autobiography reveals that emotionally he missed the constancy and security that comes from a family deeply rooted in a specific place. In his autobiography, *The Big Sea*, he confesses that his father, whom he did not love, provided the only constancy in his life because his father, at least, "stayed put" (36). On the other hand, because of his constant mobility, Hughes created families, communities, and cultures for himself wherever he went.

Hughes was determined to be part of the American literary community. He achieved and surpassed that goal and became one of literature's most important figures. Along with Zora Neale Hurston, Hughes was the artist of that era whose work has had the most critical impact on African American literature. A significant number of contemporary writers attribute their own success to the work of Hughes and Hurston.

Typical of Hughes's work on migrating African Americans is the migrant in "Bound No'th Blues." This is a fun poem and easy to use in the classroom. In this poem, Hughes tells the story of a lone traveler heading from his rural southern home to the North who feels the burden and loneliness of his travels. In a conversation with the Lord, he lays out his case:

> Goin' down the road, Lawd,
> Goin' down the road.
> Down the road, Lawd,
> Way, way down the road.
> Got to find somebody
> To help me carry this load.

Then, as was typical for most people who had seldom, if ever, stepped out of their home areas, the journey gets longer than the migrant had anticipated. So he clarifies for the Lord that he is "way, way down the road." Most of all, the migrant feels the burden of transplantation and yearns for a companion, somebody to share the burden of the journey. Hughes intends for the reader to share the lonely traveler's lament as he continues to walk and look for a friend.

> Road's in front o' me,
> Nothin' to do but walk
> Road's in front o' me
> Walk . . . an' walk . . . an' walk.
> I'd like to meet a good friend.
> To come along and talk.

We and our students are indeed surprised to find that though the migrant has walked and walked and walked "on the no'th bound road," he hasn't gotten past the Mississippi towns that aren't "fit for a hoppin' toad."

Hughes made wonderful music in his poems, librettos, and narratives, and blended the rhythms of poetry into song in his plays. He peopled his art with the lives of people he knew and some he had only heard of, and others he drew from his imagination into embodiments of love, laughter, pain, and longing that have lasted long after he died. The later years of Langston Hughes's life provided rest for the man who understood that his life had been framed and informed by contradictions and complexities that were, for the most part, out of his control. But he never let those elements interfere with his life quests. He seldom spoke of the intimate parts of his life, but he talked often yet cagily about the rest. He was articulate and artistic in the delivery of his messages. He used almost every communication forum then known: journalism, the theater, poetry, blues, jazz, fiction, opera, and even political propaganda papers. His life was not all sweet, but he embraced and loved it all. In an upbeat and positive tone in his poem "Life Is Fine," Hughes confesses that he was born for living—living a life that was as fine as wine.

IN THE CLASSROOM:
Identifying the Folk and Place in Art

In our increasingly mobile society, a significant number of our students are from "somewhere else." A few have the stability of having being born and raised in the same area as their parents, but those numbers are constantly dwindling. "Bound No'th Blues," the poem of a migrant who doesn't make much progress in his efforts to leave home, presents a wonderful opportunity to engage your students in Hughes's poetry while at the same time defining where "home" is to them.

After we read "Bound No'th Blues," I assign my students "The Negro Artist and the Racial Mountain," asking them to identify the people Hughes calls "the folk" in his essay. Then I have them jot down how they identify "the folk" in their lives. I like to tell my students that for me, "people" are persons I don't know personally, or those people I have some professional or social interaction with, but the "folk" are those people with whom I share my personal life. As a caveat, there is a tendency in this exercise to slip into a kind of relaxed writing that sounds more like "the folk" than the students. I believe in character development, and if this language is an attempt to create recognizable characters, it's fine, but I make sure that my students understand from the outset that I expect all of their papers, including this one, to reflect the kind of thinking and writing that is valued in the academic and professional worlds. In other words, one of the primary purposes in writing is to allow the audience to share the experience being described, so students need to create images that use all the senses, especially sight and sound; hence, they need to replicate their characters' speech as closely as possible. Outside the characters' own words, however, students need to be writing in Standard English.

I remind students that we do this exercise because it is important that we know, in specific terms, the characteristics of our audience when we write. We also need to be able to identify the author's audience. Hughes knew exactly who his audiences were and what would appeal to them. He knew their habits, their hopes, and their homes. Our students likewise need to identify precise audiences for their works. If you haven't already, introduce them to the concept of audience in their own writing. Students often have it in their heads that their audience is us, the teachers, those who are grading their papers. While this is true on one level, in the larger picture their audience is those people to whom they will be writing after they leave our classrooms. We need to teach students how to target those audiences.

I always keep a stack of 3" x 5" cards handy, and for this exercise I pass them out liberally. Each student gets several of these cards, and they write one description of an individual—part of their perceived folk—on each card. Then I collect the cards and shuffle them. I love having my students work collaboratively, so I put them in groups of three or four, never more than five, a group size that tends to get out of hand. Big groups also allow some individuals not to do much work. In groups of three or four, each person has to participate in order for them to come up with a product. Five minutes is enough time for this part of the exercise. This time limit forces students to get right to work; any longer than that and they start socializing. After I give each group a handful of the cards, they discuss amongst themselves the descriptions on the cards and then create a picture of "the folk" that they share with the entire class. Each group identifies its "folk" in terms as specific as those used by Hughes. We usually have a wonderful laugh because all "the folk" are different and most descriptions are pretty bizarre.

You can then give students a topic and have them write about what would be important to say to their audience if they were creating different works for their "folk." This exercise is also a good tool for having students identify who they consider to be "outsiders." Recent history, such as the school shootings at Columbine and in Minnesota, has taught us that tragedy often occurs when students feel alienated. Writing about how far down the road constitutes "somewhere else" geographically, physically, and intellectually helps students to understand one another and their individual and collective journeys. These discussions have always led to students reaching out and erasing invisible borders between them. They come to realize how artificial their differences are, that the student sitting next to them from Mississippi likes many of the same things they do. They learn that the student who stutters can draw beautiful pictures and doesn't stutter at all when he sings. They come to appreciate that they aren't the only ones who have recently moved to the area.

Personal reflection papers provide a sound foundation for the early stages of writing. I use them often to help students connect with a work before they write critical papers. They understand the experiences they have lived through that have taught them lessons. When they filter their reading through those experiences, the reading and the work itself become more meaningful. Meaning and interpretation in reading literature are often tied to emotion. The stronger the feeling, the better the reader understands the work.

I grade this exercise in two stages. I certainly respond to this exercise as an English teacher and mark grammatical and structural errors in my students' work, but at first reading I'm not as critical on response papers as on more formal papers. In fact, I have recently begun simply putting check marks in the margins if there is an error on that line. As teachers, it is our natural tendency to "correct" or "fix" our students' mistakes. Try to resist. Let students write openly and honestly about their reactions to the readings without having to worry about being marked down for incorrect grammar. I usually give this part of the exercise an X if it was well done, meaning thoroughly developed; a check for a good job; and a dash if it looked as though the student simply "blew off" the exercise. Some will. I have had my share of "I really liked this poem. It was good" responses, and I don't reward those papers with points.

In the second phase of this exercise, students use their handbooks to identify the mistake that precipitated the margin marks, if they can. This gives them multiple learning reinforcements. They have to try to figure out the error, look it up in the handbook, read the rule, write it down, and correct their paper. A few of them are stumped and can't find one or two of the errors. That's fine. Concerned students will ask me to identify the problem for them, which I freely do. The ones who want to let it go sometimes have to be called to the desk. The students then correct grammatical problems and further develop the paper for a grade. It is important, however, to let them commit their thoughts to paper in that initial "un-gussied-up" reaction.

Reactions to the readings are varied, which is normal. For the most part, students are entering into readings that have points of view and relate experiences that are alien to them. Although we should certainly talk about setting and put a reading in context for students, the response paper allows them to interpret the reading and make personal connections. My student Tracey Gray, in her first response, wrote that "Bound No'th Blues" is about a "life where people are forced to grow up too fast and miss out on their childhood completely causing a sense of rebellion to live what they weren't able to." I'm not sure I saw all of this in the poem, but my personal response isn't the point. This is what Tracey saw and articulated. This is the method she used to connect with the writings of Langston Hughes and to give them an importance and validity in her life. There are no "good" or "bad" reactions. The next phase of Tracey's response paper focused on how having to move so much because her parents kept getting transferred was hard on her education. Having students like Tracey give voice to their interpretations of the readings and connect them to their personal lives reassures me that I have created an atmosphere of safety in my classroom, where my students feel free to interpret and articulate their responses to the works in their own ways.

Sometimes I remark that a thought is underdeveloped or that the student needs to make a direct connection with something in the text. I have lost more than one fingernail trying to keep from saying, "How the heck did you come up with *this*," when there seems to be no clear or even convoluted road from the materials I assigned to students' responses. At these times, however, I rejoice in the wonderful imaginations of young people. Sometimes when I'm sitting on my deck listening to the birds call to one another across the yards and watching the squirrels play tag in the trees, one of these papers reveals its path to me. Then I know it is time to go inside.

3 I'll Build Me a World: The Harlem Renaissance

Ah, the Harlem Renaissance: bathtub gin; speakeasies; beautiful, light-brown-skinned dancing girls at the Cotton Club and Small's Paradise; "Stomping at the Savoy"; benevolent gangsters; rich White patrons paying monthly stipends to support Black writers, painters, sculptors; Black people and White people partying together in Manhattan; intellectuals, artists of all genres, and the common folk holding conversations deep into the night. These are some of the popular images of the Harlem Renaissance.

This chapter focuses largely on a description of the Harlem Renaissance so that you can help your students understand the context that shaped Hughes's writing. This wildly exciting and interesting time will undoubtedly entice you to do your own research into the era. But the social, historical, economic, and artistic impact of the Harlem Renaissance on African Americans is complex and vast. This overview provides a starting place for further research.

There were, in fact, actually two movements going on simultaneously for African Americans during this time. What I consider the "umbrella" was the New Negro Movement, which saw the migration of massive numbers of African Americans from the rural South to the North, West, Midwest, and southern urban areas. Black people were leaving agrarian lives for industrialized ones. They traded in crop income for factory paychecks and were finding new freedoms away from the neoslavery that was enveloping them in the South through sharecropping and violence. African Americans were making great political, social, and educational strides.

Within this time of social upheaval for African Americans was an unprecedented transformation in the presentation of Black arts and letters, what Langston Hughes called the *New Negro Renaissance*, a term synonymous with *Harlem Renaissance*. No longer was the need to please a larger, White reading audience the primary catalyst and controller of the content of Black literature. In his seminal essay "The Negro Artist and the Racial Mountain," Hughes argued that the mountain standing in the path of progress for the new artists was the urge to imitate Whiteness in an effort to be perceived more as Americans than as African Americans. But those artists who wanted to be seen clearly as they were circumvented that racial mountain. Hughes confessed that his work was truly racial because it derived from the life he had led. Other artists who shared his artistic philosophy felt the same way: If people, White or Black, liked the art they were producing, then good. If not, it simply did not bother the artists at all. This was the attitude of the artists of the Harlem Renaissance, an attitude founded in a new freedom to express themselves as they wished.

The New Negro Renaissance has no clear beginning or end. Some scholars have dated the Harlem Renaissance from the turn of the twentieth century until the Great Depression. Others, like the renowned cultural critic Gerald Early, identify the critical shifts in African American attitudes exemplified by heavyweight boxers Jack Johnson and Joe Louis. Discuss with your students the perceptions and receptions of the two men by the larger community and how this polarization is indicative of shifting attitudes of and toward African Americans during this time. The difference between the two men can be the subject of a classroom debate—Johnson, the symbol of an uncontrolled explosion of Blackness at the beginning of the twentieth century, and Louis, the gentleman boxer. In debating the issues, students can focus on whether and how these two boxers' positions are relevant today.

A master with his fists, Johnson beat White opponents in the ring without being lynched. He also put himself at risk by his disrespect of White women. In fact, his relationships with White women—that ultimate transgression for Black men—put his life in jeopardy. In an age when many Black men were lynched for just looking at a White woman, Johnson managed to escape despite his open violation of this and other racial taboos. He thus became, to a large degree, an iconoclastic hero to Black America.

Joe Louis, on the other hand, represents reconciliation. He was America's boxer during a time when America needed heroes. Thus his fight against Max Schmeling was not Black boxer against White boxer, but America's boxer against Germany's boxer. He served the United States in the military and represented what was good and powerful in the nation. The wide and warm acclaim he received because he won for the United States and because he served his country well against her enemies made Louis a symbol of the possibility of social cohesion between Black and White America.

Black writers adopted that same sense of excellence and pride in America as they assumed a place of literary prominence in the country. Many of the writers modeled their work after European artists, who represented "high art." Others, like Langston Hughes and Zora Neale Hurston, crafted their art around the lives of the folk. Because Hughes and Hurston are such important figures in this great literary movement, I extend the ending date of the New Negro Renaissance to about 1940, primarily because Zora Neale

Hurston's landmark book *Their Eyes Were Watching God* wasn't published until 1937. I don't extend it any further than that because writers such as Sterling Brown, Frank Marshall Davis, Richard Wright, and others who were active in the 1940s purposely disassociated themselves from Harlem and the artists of the Harlem Renaissance.

What is important in teaching the Harlem Renaissance is not the dates or even the place (Hughes and the other artists often retreated to other places they called "home"), but that Harlem was the hub of the intellectual community that evolved; also important are the transformations that took place in African American arts and letters. That world changed forever during this movement. Hughes tells us that during this time African American artists finally threw off the restraints of writing to please the intellectual and artistic palates of Whites and wrote to please themselves. This is not to say these artists were not aware of the influence and power of White publishers and patrons. They were very much aware of how much they needed the acceptance of both groups. But the context as well as the content of their art assumed more of the artists' life experiences and insights. In Harlem during this movement, artists in all mediums shared their ideas, their art, and their lives with one other.

Like most of the other artists of the era, Langston Hughes needed a world of Black people from which to draw artistic energy. He found that world in Harlem. He developed his artistry there. He chose, like Zora Neale Hurston, Black folk, Black lives, and Black music as the mode, model, and inspiration for his work.

Hughes began publishing his poems in *Crisis*, the literary magazine of the National Association for the Advancement of Colored People (NAACP). Although he did not revise most of his work and adopted for the most part a "one-write" philosophy, especially with his poetry, Hughes became successful in winning literary contests, getting published, and establishing a reputation in the literary, social, and political arenas. This can be problematic for us as teachers, when our students look to Hughes's success as a means to justify their own resistance to revising their work. We do, however, have some ammunition to thwart this counterproductive thinking. We can point them to "The Weary Blues," a poem that Hughes wrote and rewrote, polishing it to a fine luster before submitting it to the contest that catapulted him to success.

For the artists living the Harlem Renaissance, defining this movement was not an easy task. African American artist Aaron Douglas clearly delineates the task he and Langston faced in creating their powerful and "authentic Negro" art:

> Your problem Langston, my problem, no, our problem is to conceive, develop, establish an art era. Not White art painted Black. . . . No, let's bare our arms and plunge deep through laughter, through pain, through sorrow, through hope, through disappointment, into the very depths of the souls of our people and drag forth materials crude, rough, neglected. Then let's sing it, dance it, write it, paint it. Let's do the impossible. Let's create something transcendentally material, mystically objective. Earthy. Spiritually earthy. Dynamic. (Douglas qtd. in Kirschke 78, 79)

Before Hughes became part of the New Negro Renaissance, his life and habitats had none of the glamour of the life that he imagined the Negro intellectuals shared. Alain Locke, Howard University professor and self-proclaimed "midwife" to the movement, was the first to contact this fledgling poet, insisting that Hughes be included with the other younger artists. Working and living on the docks, Langston did not want the "distinguished professor from Howard, a Ph.D. at that" (*Big Sea* 93), to visit him there. After all, Hughes "knew only the people [he] had grown up with, and they weren't people whose shoes were always shined, who had been to Harvard, or who had heard Bach" (93). It was not until editor and novelist Jessie Fauset invited him to a luncheon for *Crisis* that Langston met the intelligentsia face to face. Although Hughes was impressed, he interrupted his work and his place in the movement by sailing for Europe and Asia.

His reentry into the Harlem Renaissance began almost as soon as he returned to the United States in 1924. Hughes went straight to Harlem and immersed himself in his life as a poet. He became acquainted with some of the most influential people of the time, such as poet Countee Cullen and entertainment critic Carl Van Vechten. He also renewed his connection with the NAACP. All these connections had a profound impact on his life and writing. Hughes's poetry writing continued when he left Harlem and moved to Washington, D.C., to enroll at Howard University. With no tuition money and no available scholarships, he was denied admission. The harsh winter weather and the cold treatment he experienced from African Americans in Washington were good for creativity, and Hughes wrote many poems during this period.

Those poems captured the beat and rhythm of the blues and spirituals. Langston lived and listened to the blues. He loved the places where Black folk congregated and talked and sang about life: the barbershops, barrelhouses, shouting churches, nightclubs and bars. In these places, he found the stories, the rhythms, and the people he would re-create in his work. Hughes would develop his Jesse B. Semple stories (the Simple stories) from a character he had never met but had heard about in the neighborhood bar he frequented. He intended this character to be funny as well as have far-reaching social and political implications in the stories he delivered to his readers. Hughes used humor to talk about issues as important as race relations, the atomic bomb, poverty, and religious faith. Like Mark Twain, he believed that humor was a good weapon against hypocrisy.

Hughes's career took off with a blues poem. "The Weary Blues," published by *Opportunity*, the newsmagazine of the Urban League, launched his career and established his place among the literary giants of the Harlem Renaissance. More important, he met many distinguished artists and writers of the time, including Zora Neale Hurston, Countee Cullen, Jessie Fauset, and Eric Walrond, among other young artists, and reacquainted himself with James Weldon Johnson, Alain Locke, and W. E. B. DuBois, the old guard.

These people, these folk, and these places were the tools that allowed Hughes to breathe a remarkable life into his work. In our contemporary world, where issues of difference and diversity are vigorously debated, there is much space for lessons on life and living that we can learn by reading the works of Langston Hughes and understanding the Harlem Renaissance and New Negro Movement.

IN THE CLASSROOM:
Live and Let Live in Return

As high school literature teachers, it is sometimes difficult to teach a literary movement. Students often want to link only one writer to the era, such as Shakespeare with the Elizabethan period, Jonathan Swift with the neoclassical, Phillis Wheatley with slave poetry, and Hughes with the Harlem Renaissance. Although these writers serve as prototypes for their respective eras, for a richer understanding and appreciation of literature, our students need to be able to contextualize these writers' lives with their literatures.

When we study Hughes's autobiography, we don't often have the time to commit our classes to reading the entire text, so I assign specific chapters of *The Big Sea*. I like using "When the Negro Was in Vogue" because this chapter covers the time in Hughes's life that he identifies as most important to his artistic development. My students are then afforded an opportunity to learn about the Harlem Renaissance and the New Negro Movement. There is such a wide range of topics and genres from which to choose that students can pursue their particular interests for this research.

As I discussed earlier, I view the New Negro Movement as an umbrella movement. It covers all the political, cultural, emotional, and social changes that African Americans in the United States were making at the time. No longer did Black folk feel the need to succumb to the orders of Whites, and they were taking freedom and liberties never available to them before. At least, they were taking them to the extent that a Jim Crow—i.e., legally segregated—society would let them. African Americans were moving away from the rural South to urban centers in both the North and South. They were finding means of supporting themselves that provided regular paychecks, instead of being imprisoned in the perpetual poverty of sharecropping. They were moving their families and their destinies to places where they could take care of themselves and one another. Hughes re-creates declarations made by those folk in forms that are palatable and enjoyable to a wide reading audience.

In the Harlem Renaissance, African American artists lived out the exhortations made by Hughes in "The Negro Artist and the Racial Mountain" to express themselves however they pleased.

Some chose to emulate European artists; others found their own artistic voices.

The students take away various images from their study of the New Negro Movement and the Harlem Renaissance. The response of a Congolese student in my class illustrates how Hughes speaks across cultures to the colonial experience:

> After reading "When the Negro Was in Vogue" by Langston Hughes, I could also relate to it. Mostly because my country, the Congo, was also at a point invaded by Europeans. My grandparents were not allowed to go certain places in their own country. They couldn't either say aloud what they thought about colonization.

She then went on to talk about writers in the Congo being restricted in their work during colonization, but that they were now enjoying a few freedom. I truly enjoyed sharing this student's response with the rest of the class. Although the parallel is not perfect—African Americans were not literally invaded within this country—students learn that cultural and social repression is not confined to the United States.

Langston Hughes, Countee Cullen, Zora Neale Hurston, Eric Walrond, and Aaron Douglas, among many others, were essentially creating a new aesthetic. Students readily identify with this phenomenon because they feel that their generation is creating new artistic expressions, in particular with rap and spoken word poetry. In many cases, new genres are being crafted and created. But this comparison provides a teachable moment about the evolution of art, particularly through the example of rap. While young people don't want to connect *their music* to old-school music, they learn that new art forms are never completely divorced from those that came before them. The desire to be different and new helps students identify with the young revolutionaries of the Harlem Renaissance who produced their own literary magazine *Fire!* in order to publish their art their way.

I ask my students to create their own version of *Fire!* This exercise presents valuable learning experiences for both the teacher and the students. The assignment calls for students to follow their own artistic aesthetics and produce art their way. Since I have sensitive ears and we operate under certain codes as an educational institution, my students do have to refrain from profanity. In this context, we discuss issues of appropriate language, which gives students the opportunity to reflect on their word choices and on word usage. (I am still amazed at what does not constitute inappropriate language to them.) Sometimes the classroom is autocratic, and I'm in control. Other times we vote. With the exception of those moments when they want to use inappropriate language, the students are allowed to express themselves however they see fit in this magazine. They can submit articles, poems, short stories, art, and so forth. They can choose to create new art forms or they can fall back on established forms. Some have created a hybrid of several forms. One student created a rather primitive poster with cutouts from magazines but then recorded a rap song that talked about the different images on the poster. Another gave a Bratz doll voice and had her "talk" about the way young girls were being treated. A young man wrote a three-character play in which the "hard-headed" boy character only rapped, which infuriated his mother and girlfriend.

Other students, like Robert Hotchkiss, decided to respond to Hughes's life in the Harlem Renaissance by writing poetry. Robert hooked onto the images in "When the Negro Was in Vogue" for this work. In his explanation of the poem, he quotes Hughes:

"the gay and sparkling life of the so-called Negro Renaissance of the 20s was not so gay and sparkling beneath the surface as it looked" (*Big Sea* 227).

The Performance

I grin, dance, and sing
With diminishing dignity.
The façade of my long smile
Will only last another short while.

The black hats and coattails
Contrast with their skin so pale.
They come from uptown
To gawk at this man so brown.

They fervently clap and laugh
For their own pleasures behalf
If the ignorant only knew
How I know them straight through.
This club was once free of colorless skeptics
And enjoyed by crowds much more ethnic.
Now my artistic song and dance
Is dictated by their deep finance.

Another long and shallow night
Until the dimming of Harlem's bright lights.
—*Robert Hotchkiss*

This, of course, came after our class discussion that *gay* did not mean "homosexual" in the Harlem Renaissance; it meant "happy." The students then felt free to use the word in their responses.

Another student, Steve Doane, who is Jewish, was inspired to return to a short story he had imagined but never written. His story, which he didn't title, takes place in 1920s Detroit, a time when alcohol was illegal. During this time, a Jewish gang ruled most of the alcohol sales and bootlegging. I have taken what I have learned about short stories and the elements that short stories have into my own short story. I have characters, a plot, a conflict, and even my meter changes pace through out the story. I was able to complete this because of what I learned and from the examples of a [Hughes] short story that I read, "The Blues I'm Playing."

Steve's strategy of changing African American gangsters into Jewish ones demonstrates that he was able to absorb the story and then filter it through his own experiences and his imagination.

4 The Sounds and Rhythms of Life: Movin' On

As high school teachers, you are working with a student population that spends a great deal of time with music—playing it, singing it, dancing to it, composing it, thinking about it. Hughes offers us a wonderful forum for teaching poetry through his poems, many of which replicate the rhythmic patterns of music, particularly the blues. Hughes's love for music is obvious not only in his blues poetry but also in his use of the free-flow forms that mimic the cadences of jazz to establish the tempo of the poem. He also loved the opera and musical theater and wrote librettos and musicals. Helping students make the connection between Hughes's poems and music enriches their engagement with both.

The Blues

The blues beat the rhythms of a people in motion, people living active, vibrant lives. Most of the time, the blues are about problems; however, they almost always end in triumph or at least reconciliation. The initial reaction of younger students is that the blues are "old folks" music; as one of my students put it, "the blues are about cats and dogs and girlfriends running away." But after they spend a few minutes saying good riddance to the things they would like to have run away in their lives, the students are ripe to hear the rhythm of the blues. Then they are ready to hear that Hughes sings songs of success as he emulates the sounds and the rhythms of the folk. The jazz and blues cadences in his poetry set the beat for the lyrics, capturing the meter of the lives of the folk. When the folk are happy, they whirl, twirl, and throw their arms wide to the wonder of their lives; when they are sad, the tempo slows and they lament having moved only a few feet.

Hughes particularly liked and used the blues form in his writing. Share with your students some of Hughes's experiences with the blues. For example, just tinkering around one day, he wrote his first blues poem, "The Weary Blues," which is about a piano player in Harlem. The poem became special to him, and he took a soft word-cloth and polished it to perfection. "The Weary Blues" is also special because it talks of the blues in relation to the poet's life. While he was observing and absorbing life in Harlem, Hughes watched a piano player in a cabaret whose music captured the rhythm of the lazy sway of jazz musicians. This rhythm became an integral part of "The Weary Blues," as well as of much of Hughes's work. To the melodies and lyrics of blues pieces he heard as a young man wandering on Lenox Avenue, Hughes added the first blues verse he had ever heard in Lawrence, Kansas, when he was a little boy:

> I got de weary blues
> And I can't be satisfied . . .
> I ain't happy no mo'
> And I wish that I had died.

Then he shifts language. The polished poet ends the piece after the musician goes to bed. Hughes privileges readers by allowing us to know what's going on with the blues singer after he leaves Lenox Avenue:

> The singer stopped playing and went to bed.
> While the Weary Blues echoed through his head.
> He slept like a rock or a man that's dead.

I find that few students can resist sounding like a blues artist when they read the poems aloud. The rhythm refuses to be stifled. In the third stanza of "Bound No'th Blues," the repetition and cadence of the poem forces them to hear and even sing the blues:

> Hates to be lonely,
> Lawd, I hates to be sad.
> Says I hates to be lonely,
> Hates to be lonely and sad,
> But ever friend you finds seems
> Like they try to do you bad.

So that my students can connect the blues rhythm to Hughes's poetry, I usually bring a B. B. King CD to class. Hearing King belt out the blues and wail his anguish on Lucille, his guitar, also helps dispel the notion that the blues are depressing songs. Hughes says that "the mood of the blues is almost always despondency, but when they are sung people laugh" (qtd. in Rampersad's introduction to *The Big Sea* xxv). I promise that your classroom will erupt in laughter when your students hear some of the songs, just as they will laugh when they read some of Hughes's poetry. Along with the music of his poetry, Hughes offers humorous and poignant dialectal conversations of the folk as they explore and explain their new lives. Minnie, for example, in "Minnie sings her Blues," tells us that she and her man go to the cabaret to get out of the snow. But when she confesses that the real reason she goes is to dance with her husband, which keeps the other girls away from him, students really engage with the poem.

Suffering, Injustice, and Politics

Hughes braids the emotions of the blues into poems about the injustices that Black people have suffered. His poetry is filled with characters who find their way into a new life, in a new time, and in a new space. Part of this new life involved the interaction, on newly arriving from the South, with White people on a level that was completely foreign to them. These characters are at first astounded at the power they think Blacks have in the North. Then they are reminded that the scales of justice are not balanced in their favor, not even in the judicial system, where justice means "just us"—just Black people are punished. Hughes identifies justice in his poem of the same name as a blind goddess with two festering sores where her eyes used to be. More important, he identifies that blindness as something that all Black people know about, "a thing to which we blacks are wise."

"Ballad of the Landlord" explores another injustice the new migrants suffer, in this case at the hands of absentee or ineffective landlords who let their properties deteriorate once the apartments are occupied by African Americans. The poem describes in vivid detail the tenant's experience with the physical deterioration of the property, as well as the victimization of the tenant—who ultimately goes to jail simply for standing up to the landlord.

"Ballad of the Landlord" is also important as an example of Hughes's political position. Hughes believed that all art was propaganda, so he used his work, especially his blues poetry, to promote the causes of the underclass. He used the rhythm of the blues, especially repetition, to reinforce key points, such as the powerlessness of African Americans in a judicial system in which a White man's word is always taken over theirs, and in which those people who are fighting to correct social inequities are also treated unfairly. Hughes also created characters who are symbols of freedom and who find the power to subvert the legal system that controls them.

To help students get a better understanding of Hughes's poems of injustice, introduce them to W. E. B. DuBois, who talks of the "double-consciousness" or duality with which Black people live: the tension between the essentialist, negative stereotype that others have of them and their own understanding of themselves (37–44). Hughes infuses this double consciousness into his characters, who can manipulate White people into perceiving them as naive and childlike at best, and stupid and lazy at worst. In reality, these characters know that they are sophisticated, intelligent, cunning, and hard-working adults. Hughes, like other writers such as Toni Morrison, points to the skill with which African Americans have learned to operate in this binary. They have, in fact, honed a well-crafted subversive quality as a means to outwit White people and to survive. Through this subversiveness, African Americans were able to earn money, educate their children, and accumulate property under the noses of unsuspecting Whites, who were constantly legislating against them.

Race

Students engage with powerful events and processes in Black history through Hughes's poetry, which opens their eyes to historical and current racism. Hughes depicts the horror of rural southern (racial) cruelty in poems like "Song for a Dark Girl":

> Way Down South in Dixie
> . . . .
> They hung my black young lover
> To a cross roads tree.

. . . .

Way Down South in Dixie
. . . .
Love is a naked shadow
        On a gnarled and naked tree.

This poem tells of a lynching and the pain that comes from losing a loved one to violence, but it also touches on the issue of religious faith. After her lover is lynched, the narrator—the Dark Girl— loses faith in the power of prayer. Blacks have often looked to Christianity to sustain them, but Hughes points to the failure of a "white Lord Jesus" who, the poet suggests, doesn't hear the prayers of Black supplicants, especially those from "Way Down South in Dixie." Students will be moved by the powerful image of the Dark Girl seeing her lover reduced to a "naked shadow" hanging from a "gnarled and naked tree." The stark simplicity of the poem, along with the sorrowful blues cadence, allows the readers to feel the Dark Girl's grief.

Jazz

In contrast to that of his blues poetry, the rhythm of Hughes's jazz poems assumes an upbeat cadence. But here again, Hughes complicates the joy with the undertones of sorrow. In "Dream Boogie," for example, he writes in a snappy rhythm, and his narrator, a southern migrant settled in Harlem, refuses to acknowledge that life in the North isn't all he had hoped for. It is, in fact, a "dream deferred."

Dream Boogie
Langston Hughes

Good morning, daddy!
Ain't you heard
The boogie-woogie rumble
Of a dream deferred?

Listen closely:
You'll hear their feet
Beating out and beating out a—

> *You think*
> *It's a happy beat?*

Listen to it closely:
Ain't you heard
Something underneath
Like a—
> *What did I say?*

Sure,
I'm happy!
Take it away!
> *Hey, pop!*
> *Re-bop!*
> *Mop!*

> *Y-e-a-h!*

A close reading of this poem allows students to uncover the para-doxical nature of the narrator's emotions, one that typifies much of the Black experience. Through the rhythm of his words, the narrator professes to a good time and happiness, but the words themselves, in particular *dream deferred*, *beating out*, and the mysterious *something underneath*, belie his happiness. Masking sadness in musical poetry is a strategy that Hughes uses to link the optimistic promise that leaving the South gave the migrants to the disappointment they found in the North.

Hughes not only builds bridges between the lives of the folk in the South and the reality of their experiences in the North, but he is also concerned with the lives of people in different socioeconomic classes. He writes of Black people who need to throw rent parties to pay their monthly rent, as well as of the long white fingers that belong to his rich White patron, Mrs. R. Osgood Mason, who cut coupons in her Park Avenue apartment.

Ultimately, despite the sorrow and the injustice, by writing about Blacks and Whites and the rich and the poor, Hughes suggests that the distance between people of all stations is not as great as it would appear. His poem "Question [1]" brings the point home:

> When the old junk man Death
> Comes to gather up our bodies
> And toss them into the sack of oblivion,
> I wonder if he will find
> The corpse of a white multi-millionaire
> Worth more pennies of eternity
> Than the black torso of
> A Negro cotton-picker?

Hughes emphasizes that racial strife is a waste of time and energy when life will end the same for all of us. Instead, we should be reveling in the glorious triumphs of our lives. His poetry urges the reader to feel the rich and varied rhythms of life, and in teaching Hughes I try to emphasize this point.

IN THE CLASSROOM:
Confronting Racial Attitudes—Inner and Outer Spaces

Poems and stories about lynching are difficult for me to discuss with my students. It is painful for me and for them to deal with senseless violence. You should be prepared for emotional moments and allow yourself time to think through how you will deal with the subject. You will find that students who often remain unemotional about drive-by shootings and "going postal" get emotionally invested in any discussion about lynching. For me, the best way to approach the subject is on an intellectual basis, through discussing historical context.

At first, students may have difficulty imagining the period in which these events occurred. The early twentieth century in which Hughes sets his work is ancient history to them, so you will need to engage your students with this era that to them seems distant and irrelevant. When they dismiss events as happening so long ago and ask questions like "How could people do that?," I have only to remind them of James Byrd in Texas who was dragged behind a truck until his body parts scattered along the road. Introduce them to Lucille Clifton's powerful poem "jasper texas 1998," in which Byrd's head narrates the event. I then give students more history about lynching, telling them that dragging was a common form of lynching in the 1890s and the 1920s, as well as now. I bring my copy of James Allen's *Without Sanctuary* to class, not to show them the pictures of the corpses dangling from trees, but to show them the faces of the people in the crowds and the postcards they made of the lynching to send to family members who were not able to attend. In the discussion that follows, we talk about how racism and racial hatred are taught traits, not inherent. The pictures of smiling mothers holding their babies beneath a burned body bring the point home.

I like to give my students different ranges of years to research for social and political conditions. The students who have 1619 to 1775, for example, will be writing on colonial slavery in America. The next range is 1776–1863, which covers antebellum slavery; 1866–1877 is the Reconstruction period; and so on. Students research the social conditions of Blacks and who the major American writers are in the era. Working in groups makes this research less stressful and more fun. Students usually divide the research into areas such as social rituals, major religions, what people did to make their livings, size of families, etc. When they finally compile their research, they have re-created an era. Taking this approach to background research means I am not forced to commit large blocks of class time to teaching African American history. Instead, my students focus on one era but learn about many others. They also connect writers such as Hawthorne and Twain to the times.

After each group has presented its research to the entire class, I move to the most positive part of this exercise, the reaction papers. The students often talk about themselves and how they have overcome the racism their parents still hold near and dear and have tried to teach them. Other students believe that racism is completely absent from their lives and their environs. Devin Elias writes:

> Racism is a horrible thing towards any one. Fortunately, we live in a day and age where it has changed for the better, but it still exists in some parts of the United States. I grew up in the South and there is still racism there like you would not be-

lieve. It makes me angry to see acts of racism committed against anyone. I hate to see one particular race purposely suppress that of another. Those people are bigots; they are heartless things that we should not even call human. Langston Hughes left me feeling angry . . . not necessarily because of what he wrote, but because of the feelings it brought out in me.

As teachers, we probably cannot undo the damage already done by parents and communities that have passed on racist views, but we can use this opportunity to study Hughes's poetry as a way to confront this sensitive and emotionally charged issue. We can't just say "Poor little Dark Girl. What a shame" and then move on to the next poem. We have to allow our students to feel whatever they feel when they experience the poem. That is the only way to read poetry.

In discussions of these physical, social, and economic gaps between White and Black, rich and poor, students express themselves any way they want. Seth Fausset responded to Hughes through his own poem and then commented on his response:

> I think I wrote it [his poem "Skin"] because I think we look at the way God made us wrong. We judge outward appearance too much. I think we look at it as a suggestion about a person's inner self when it really doesn't. It might tell you small things about a person. But I think the real details of our lives cut a little deeper than skin.

Then Seth takes a lesson from Langston Hughes's "The Negro Artist and the Racial Mountain," ending with, "Anyway, I wrote it and that's that. Hope you like it but oh well if you don't. It's mine in the end." I did like it, so I'm sharing it with you.

Skin

Nothing fits me like my skin.
Familiar, snug, warm
Sometimes it itches
Sometimes I want to take it off
Run naked and free
Free from its wear and tear
Free from its monotonous use

A man shot himself today
Guess his fit a little too tight
Couldn't wait till he got home

Sometimes I admire other people's attire
Like a nice coat on a department store rack
I compare theirs to mine
      Mine is too short
      It's too thick in all the wrong places

Sometimes I see other people's that don't fit so well
It makes me appreciate mine a little more

Some days I'm happy in mine
Some days not.

In the end
Nothing fits me like my skin.

                               —Seth Fausset

Another student, Jasmine Brown, found inspiration in the writer who claimed the role of voice for the folk who had none:

I truly respect Langston Hughes for what he did because he was not afraid to voice his opinion regardless of the consequences. His works were from the heart and told stories of black folk across the nation. Those who are truly great inspire others to greatness; Langston Hughes did that, without a doubt. . . . He opened the doors for others to speak and write about how they felt. I am thankful for the role models like Langston Hughes that we have been given to look up to and realize that you can do anything you set your mind to, regardless of the opposition.

I am truly thankful that Hughes's work inspires my students to lift their heads and realize that no one can stop them once they set their minds to succeed. The distance between failure and success is in the depth of their hearts.

5 A Novel Affair: *Not without Laughter*

■ ■

Langston Hughes wrote two novels, *Not without Laughter* and *Tambourines to Glory*. The latter is best known in its second form as a play. I focus on *Not without Laughter* in this chapter because it is better written and more accessible to students. A young boy's coming-of-age story, *Not without Laughter* strongly appeals to girls as well as boys. In addition to the young boy, Sandy, Hughes follows the life of a young woman, Sandy's Aunt Harriett, through her trials and tribulations as she grows into triumphant womanhood. The novel is set in the early 1900s, and both Sandy and Harriett experience many of the same difficulties as those of young people in the twenty-first century. Today, ignorance, racism, sexism, drugs, and a host of negative forces work even more strongly on our students.

Not without Laughter as a Reflection of Hughes's Family

In *The Big Sea*, Hughes confesses that he didn't have a real family, so he made up one for *Not without Laughter*, a semiautobiographical novel set in Stanton, the fictional version of Lawrence, Kansas (303). The truth is that the characters closely resemble Hughes's real family. This novel is especially useful for the classroom because the individual characters are so richly developed that we feel we know them personally. Encourage your students to search for the parallels between the characters and the people in Hughes's life, provided there is time in the unit for students to do some research on Hughes's personal life. Students will discover that the character loosely based on Hughes himself is the boy-child Sandy, who is being raised by his grandmother, Aunt Hagar. Even though she is mother and grandmother to the primary characters in the story, everyone in Stanton, including her own family, calls her "Aunt Hagar" out of respect for her role as the community healer and helper. Hughes, as we know, was raised by his grandmother, Mary Leary Langston, also a proud, well-respected woman in her community. Hughes's mother Carrie is mirrored in Sandy's mother, Annjee, who sacrifices her relationship with her only child to follow her husband, as did Carrie. Carrie, like Annjee, later reconciles with her child, whose help she needs to partially support her with his earnings from work on the boat docks.

The Redemptive Power of Music

In *Not without Laughter*, once again you can use music as an entry point into the work. The redemptive power of music is a powerful theme in this novel. Jimboy, Sandy's father, who was born in the South and partially raised by parents who couldn't claim any kind of social standing, makes beautiful music. Ask your students to identify the role of music in the lives not only of Jimboy but also of Annjee, her younger sister Harriett, and Aunt Hagar. It is music that makes Jimboy acceptable to the community, as it does Harriett. Through Jimboy's and Harriett's music, Hughes makes visible the lives of a people whose socioeconomic conditions don't allow for much entertainment and culture outside of their own creativity; yet they use their gifts of music to make their lives bearable and even enjoyable. Jimboy's guitar playing and Harriett's dancing and singing revitalize the lives of everyone in the family, including Aunt Hagar, who pretends to hate the music. We even catch Aunt Hagar rocking on the porch or in the yard in the evenings as she listens to Jimboy play and Harriett sing. Music is the vehicle through which Jimboy finds a place in the family and respectability in the community; it moves Aunt Hagar, who makes him play her favorite spirituals. Much later in the story, music saves Sandy from a life in hot, small, rented rooms in big cities, working for small change so that he can take care of his mother after Jimboy abandons her to fight in the war.

Harriett is also saved by music. She runs away from a life in Stanton, which probably would have led to her ruin, to become a successful blues singer. In telling Harriett's story, Hughes uses music to provide the resolution. Harriett's music allows her to earn the money that makes it possible for Sandy to return to school, as he so desperately wants.

The ending of *Not without Laughter* encourages an exploration of happily-ever-after stories. Although more sophisticated readers may find the ending a bit too pat, students generally respond to the romantic aspect. The novel has the appeal of a Horatio Alger story, a formula that students can critically analyze. From poverty and prostitution, Harriett rises to be "Princess of the Blues." When she shows up in their town, Annjee and Sandy put together their little money, mostly small change, to go hear her sing. For their sacrifice, they are able to meet with Harriett, who provides the money that in a sense saves Sandy's life. One student's response to the story at this point was that Annjee and Sandy had the "hookup," meaning that they could have shown up at the club and been given free entry on the basis of their connection to the star of the show. But they didn't. This provides a teachable moment. Students can speculate about how the effect of the story would have differed if Annjee and Sandy had indeed chosen to take advantage of their connection. Students can also identify the ways in which Hughes explores the value of sacrifice in this story and then present arguments for and against their conclusions.

Ask students to explore how, with Jimboy gone, Hughes brings this story back to the theme of music through Harriett. As they trace Harriett's life through her migration to various cities, her bad behavior, and her success, they discover that music is her salvation. Even Sandy and Annjee are returned to their roots through music, as Hughes takes them down a side street, where the music of a southern-inspired church draws their attention. Symbolically, they return to the church revivals of Stanton and Aunt Hagar's teachings. With the story's ending, Hughes targets his audience of Black readers perfectly. He has the voices of the elders, "vibrant and steady like a stream of living faith" (299), refresh their souls. And for himself, a man who felt abandoned by Jesus that fateful night in Kansas when he sat on the mourner's bench with the other children waiting for a religious conversion that never came, Hughes ends with the words of an old spiritual, "An' we'll understand it better by an' by!"

The Historical Context

Through *Not without Laughter*, Hughes provides a rich history of the times. In our mobile society, our students are sometimes hard-pressed to understand why people who wanted to move away from hard times and violent places didn't just do it, especially when the $21 weekly salary of the average Black man in Harlem is for the most part throwaway money for our students. This gives us a moment to talk about relative prices and economic change. I also like to point out that even today many people find themselves in desperate situations and feel hopeless about moving beyond them. This always seems to strike a chord with some of the students.

In setting this novel at the time of the Great Depression and the massive migration of African Americans from the rural Deep South to primarily the urban North, Hughes reveals the invisible yet rigid barriers to mobility. Students can certainly be encouraged to research the economic, political, and social conditions of the era, but Hughes gives us much good historical information as well, filtered through his eyes and experience. Students learn about this era through Jimboy's life, which is a proverbial catch-22. He is a skilled craftsman and a hard worker when he can get work; yet, because he is Black, he can rarely find work and can't keep it when he does. You can use this opportunity to discuss institutional racism in labor unions and other organizations that closed their doors to Black Americans.

Mobility and Migration

Not without Laughter captures the mobility and migration that marked the history of Black folk in the United States during this period. For the many people who shared Jimboy's frustration, the only solution was to keep moving. If small towns like Lawrence, Kansas, or other comparable places wouldn't allow African Americans to grow socially or financially or even to make sustenance wages, other places beckoned. The industrial North was the most enticing place, with its promise of factory paychecks. But movement wasn't an automatic panacea. The migrants found that the freedom and autonomy they were looking for wasn't freely accessible in many of these new places.

The train became a standard trope in African American literature, especially of this era, because it symbolized the journey to selfhood. You can use the image of the train to teach students about the power of metaphor. The long, forlorn sound of the train whistle represents the deep need to leave the confines of life wherever it is and see new parts of the world. It has the same emotional effect and sad sound as "Taps" played at a military funeral. In most cases, it carries the same sense of finality and grief. Jimboy, portrayed as a traveling man, stops whatever he is doing whenever he hears a train whistle.

The Character of Black Folk

Although Hughes's characters are compelled to move North, they do so at a cost: they lose a significant part of their souls. This trade-off is a repeated theme in many of his works, including the poems "Song for a Dark Girl" and "Harlem 1." In *Not without Laughter*, when Jimboy breaks his guitar on a crowded bus, Hughes foreshadows Jimboy's end. The character cannot survive without the most important piece of his being—his music. Jimboy is essentially lost to the story from that point on. We never hear his voice again.

Sandy's character offers teachers an opportunity to discuss Hughes's ability to create a complex character deeply interconnected with Black culture. Sandy connects his emotional self to the individual who still has music: "I'm more like Harriett. . . . I want to do something for myself, by myself. . . . Free" (289). In giving Sandy this moment of recognition, Hughes also makes a case for racial pride and criticizes people like his own father, James Hughes, who believe that being lifted from the socioeconomic conditions of the masses of the folk requires an adoption of Whiteness. "I want a house to live in, too, when I'm older. . . . But I wouldn't want to be like Tempy's friends—or her husband, dull and colorless, putting all his money away in a white bank, ashamed of colored people" (289). Sandy's declaration contrasts with the advice of Hughes's own father, who admonished his son not to live in the United States "with niggers like a nigger" (*Big Sea* 62).

Hughes emphasizes Black pride through Sandy's character and through Sandy's critique of the "colorless" Mr. Siles, who insults the folk and their music, saying, "A lot of minstrels—that's all niggers are! . . . Clowns, jazzers, just a band of dancers—that's why they never have anything. Never be anything but servants to the white people" (289). Hughes speaks through Sandy, who sees Mr. Siles and his friends as practically transparent, "colorless," neither Black nor White, and whose words have the power of vapor. Through Sandy's memories of the people he loved, the people with form and substance, Hughes reveals the innate dignity of his people:

> Clowns! Jazzers! Band of dancers! . . . Harriett! Jimboy! Aunt Hagar! . . . A band of dancers!! . . . Sandy remembered his grandmother whirling around in front of the altar at revival meetings in the midst of the other sisters, her face shining with light, arms outstretched as though all the cares of the world had been cast away; Harriett in the back yard under the apple-tree, eagle-rocking in the summer evening to the tunes of the guitar; Jimboy singing. . . . But was that why Negroes were poor, because they were dancers, jazzers, clowns! . . . The other way round would be better: dancers because of their poverty; singers because they suffered; laughing all the time because they must forget. . . . It's more like that, thought Sandy. (289–90)

You might point out to students that Hughes doesn't give his characters the option of returning to Stanton. Inevitably, the characters move on and continue with their lives elsewhere, continuing the pattern of mobility.

Teachers can help students make connections between the characters in *Not without Laughter* and characterizations of African Americans in Hughes's poems. In fact, Hughes extends the images of Black characters in *Not without Laughter* to fully describe his people in the poem "Laughers," which was originally published in *Crisis* magazine as "My People."

Laughers
Langston Hughes

Dream-singers,
Story-tellers,
Dancers,
Loud laughers in the hands of Fate—
      My people.
Dish-washers
Elevator-boys,
Ladies' maids,
Crap-shooters,
Cooks,
Waiters,
Jazzers,
Nurses of babies,
Loaders of ships,
Rounders,
Number writers,
Comedians in vaudeville
And band-men in circuses—
Dream-singers all,—
      My people.
Story-tellers all,—
My people.
      Dancers—
God! What dancers!
      Singers—
God! What singers!
Singers and Dancers
Dancers and laughers
      Laughers?
Yes, laughers . . . laughers . . . laughers—
Loud-mouthed laughers in the hands
      Of fate.

Hughes gives Sandy that same recognition:

> A band of dancers. . . . Black dancers—captured in a white world. . . . Dancers of the spirit, too. Each black dreamer a captured dancer of the spirit. . . . Aunt Hagar's dreams for Sandy dancing far beyond the limitations of their poverty, of their humble station in life, of their dark skins. (290)

Hughes makes it clear in his work that music and art and laughter are the salvation of souls and the foundations of cultures.

IN THE CLASSROOM:
Let Each One Teach One

The marvel of assigning students Hughes's works and having them respond creatively is that they produce exciting work themselves. Because Hughes wrote in many genres, he is the perfect writer for the following exercise. I create a list of about twenty Hughes poems, another list comprising three chapters from his novel *Not without Laughter*, another with a chapter from his autobiography *The Big Sea*, another with a couple of the Jesse B. Semple stories, and another with two other short stories. As students leave the classroom, I hand each of them one of the lists. The randomness of who gets which list keeps me from having to deal with requests: "I like poetry best"; "Don't give me the poetry packet. It's too hard to understand," etc. Students are to read the material and be prepared to work in a group.

Their assignment is to teach the genre on the list to the rest of the class using the Hughes material as their foundation. The benefits of this approach are many. When students take responsibility for their own learning, I do less lecturing. And when each group becomes familiar with one of the genres and teaches it to the class, everyone's learning is much richer than if I were telling them the information. By focusing on one writer who wrote in different genres, students can see how the approaches differ. Finally, students do much more work as teachers than as students. They make charts; create PowerPoint presentations; bring in videos; and play *Jeopardy!*, *Who Wants to be a Millionaire*, and similar games in which they formulate questions from their presentations that the class has to answer. They often bring in candy as a reward for the "winners." One student's mother made a delicious flag cake for her son's presentation on Hughes's political works. Though I certainly don't encourage all the extras, the students tend to go above and beyond the requirements when they are the teachers.

The students who are not presenting at the time write evaluations of their peers' presentations. I remind them to pay close attention to the presentations and stay focused. They get ten points or less depending on the quality of their evaluations. "It was a good presentation" is worth about one point. Good critical analyses are worth ten points. Awarding points gives the students' work value and encourages them to do a good critical analysis. I do not share the evaluator's name with the presenters, although I do share the positive comments and turn the negative criticisms into positives by rewording them as helpful hints for subsequent presentations.

Every semester I have students do class presentations over different aspects of the class content. Each set of presentations gets better. Students quickly come to understand what types of presentation forums lend themselves to a good group dynamic and which ones don't. What I never allow is for one person to speak while three others lean against the chalkboard. The presentation has to involve some sort of group interaction. In the initial presentations, a typical forum would be the students sitting behind a table as a panel and each one talking for a couple of minutes about some aspect or theme in the work. Then they might break out for quiz show–type interaction with the class. Of course, you run the risk of students asking for questions from the class just so they can stretch out their time. In such a case, you can intervene to refocus on the presenters. By the last sessions, students come up with much more creative forums. One group created a breaking news show with an anchor at the desk and reporters "in the field" interviewing "witnesses." Another held a mock court case in which the "writer" was being tried for creating a flawed character. One surprisingly interesting approach was a writer's workshop with the students acting as alumni of the workshop and informing the class—the future participants—of the value of understanding a writer and his or her work.

I always insist that students provide an outline for both me and the class that covers the main points they are going to raise in their presentation. This keeps the group, me, and the rest of the class focused. I also do not give too many instructions. I set time limits (usually fifteen minutes), insist on full participation, and implore them to bring out the central points no matter what their forum, but I let them determine the format. Students are far more imaginative than I am.

In addition to the group presentation, each student has to write a personal response essay to one of the works in their packet. These personal responses are quite varied. In one class, the two chapters of *Not without Laughter* I used were "Dance" and "Carnival." In her response paper, Jennifer Quinn wrote:

The carnival also had a strong religious overtone, how the young middle-aged crowd was at the carnival while the other older people were at the religious thing. This reminded me of SOR (School of Religion) which is where parents send their kids to learn how to be a good Catholics once a week, since I was not in normal catholic school (thank goodness). I hated school of religion because I had to go sit in a stupid classroom every Sunday evening while all of the other kids my age got to play outside or do their own thing. Plus, I really don't think I got anything out of SOR.

These pieces also evoked personal childhood memories for Jon VanMaren:

As I read about Mingo it reminded me of a friend in high school named Matt Monroe. Matt has the biggest and whitest smile that really stands out next to his dark skin. In addition to having a big white smile like Mingo that they both reveal a lot, Matt also became wrestling state champion this year, so naturally, he is strong.

And:

In "Carnival" Sandy steps on a nail and has to tough it out at the carnival or else he couldn't have gone. This reminds me of camping because I would always get a cut or burn and just have to deal with it the rest of the camping trip. And since we were camping our bandages were primitive like the piece of fat they tie as a remedy for the hole in Sandy's foot.

Another student, Jason Eisberg, identified with Sandy:

The character Sandy reminded me in some ways of myself. It seemed that the most dilemmas and struggles were in relation to that character. That is the way I view my own life at times. It seems that every corner there is something to worry about and fear is around. While the types of dangers and fears are different, they still probably both provoke the same types of feelings.

Hughes is a master at provoking feelings with which everyone can identify. There is something in this novel—even though the characters are of a different time, live in a different place, and face different social conditions—with which our students can identify. While it may seem like a reach to connect Aunt Hagar's tying fat on Sandy's foot to primitive camping bandages, such connections are immediate for our students. The family Hughes created in *Not without Laughter* transcends Stanton in the early twentieth century to illuminate the lives of Americans living anywhere in the United States today.

6 Pullin' in the Nets: The Autobiography

The Big Sea is a marvelous text for teaching autobiography as a genre, but because it is a long book, you will probably need to select a few chapters for study, especially if you're also planning to teach Hughes's poetry and fiction. Literary critics have argued about the exact genre that Hughes employs here, memoir or autobiography, but for the classroom teacher, these discussions are truly academic and probably not relevant to your high school students. If you do want to read more about the differences between these genres, John Edgar Tidwell offers a detailed discussion of this point in *Livin' the Blues* (Davis), as does Arnold Rampersad in his introduction to *The Big Sea*.

For teachers of autobiography, Hughes actually provides two choices: *I Wonder as I Wander* and *The Big Sea*, the latter of which we address in this text. The rich tapestry of Hughes's life story, from birth to midthirties, unfolds in this self-revelation: adventure, art, music, poetry, and people—shady characters, as well as fun ones.

Hughes uses his imagination and creativity to craft a past that selectively tells his story. With reference to the title of this book, he explains:

> Life is a big sea
> full of many fish.
> I let down my nets
> and pull.

The Big Sea is a good way to introduce your students to the personal elements in Hughes's work as well as to his life. As they read parts of his autobiography side by side with his creative writings, students make connections between the life and the work, learning simultaneously about the life and the times of an incredibly exciting and interesting man.

A Selective Story

Although he talks much about his life, Hughes refuses to open his nets to reveal his intimate history. *The Big Sea* recounts little about his love life; instead, Hughes draws attention to other dimensions of his life. Students learn that he spent time "teaching English in Mexico, truck gardening in Staten Island, [being] a seaman, a doorman, a cook, a waiter in Paris night clubs or in hotels and restaurants, a clerk at the Association for the Study of Negro Life and History, a bus boy at the Wardman Park in Washington" (335) and that he won literary awards and scholarships. It's enlightening for students to see how Hughes struggled to become a writer—how, no matter what the cost, his determination to succeed triumphed over the obstacles.

Hughes starts this autobiography with a rite of passage into manhood. He leans over the rail of the old freighter that is about to launch him into a new life as a sailor and throws all his books overboard. These books symbolize Hughes's early life. He is twenty-one, feeling grown, and he throws away those things that connect him most closely to his childhood. As the ship sails, his old life slips far behind him. Students may not consciously realize that they too go through rites of passage. This is a moment, particularly if you have diverse students, to talk about different cultural rites of passage, as well as those that students experience in their peer groups. If you haven't done so already, introduce them to the use of symbolism, relating it to Hughes's gesture of throwing his books overboard. Ask students to identify and write a one-page description of a rite of passage in their own lives that includes symbolic gestures.

Using details selectively is something all students must learn to do when they write, and Hughes is a good model. He writes about the history of the wider world, his fascination with socialism, his interrogation before the McCarthy commission, but he carefully chooses what he tells. Let students critique Hughes's choices. How much can they construct of Hughes the writer? Of Hughes the lover? The socialist? Which details are most telling?

In some instances, we as readers are forced to believe Hughes when he tells us that his early life is now behind him. But our reactions reflect Samuel Taylor Coleridge's "willing suspension of disbelief," because it is hard to completely believe Hughes. After all, as a skilled writer, in a genre in which the writer has to confess his personal secrets, isn't he obligated to tell us *everything*? Obviously not. Langston Hughes has none of that my-life-is-an-open-book-so-read-on attitude. With three exceptions, in fact, he doesn't confess or analyze the events of his early life.

Encourage students to look at what Hughes reveals of his early years and ask them to track these events as they resurface in Hughes's fiction and poetry. The first significant episode is his religious "conversion" when he was a child living with Auntie Reed. As in the poem "Dark Girl," he lays bare his own loss of faith in Jesus. He allows us to see the child crying desperately all night, waiting for the promise of comfort from religion and not getting it. Reading this section, students come to understand that this is an especially painful revelation for Hughes to make because the Reeds represented a family and a real life to Hughes. He felt abandoned by parents, his grandmother was dead, and he had no siblings (except, later, a stepbrother of whom we hear little). At that time, the Reeds constituted his family. Of them, he writes, "For me, there have never been any better people in the world. I loved them very much" (*Big Sea* 18).

Hughes's second confession involves the visit he had with his father when Langston was a teenager. Hughes came to realize that his father, whom he describes as the only stable element in his life because his father "at least stayed put" (36), was materialistic and racist and hated Negroes, the exact opposite of what Langston needed and wanted in a father. Your teenage students will be interested to learn about this conflict between a child and his parent, which was complicated by Hughes's father's hatred of his own people. Hughes admits that once he recognized the truth of his father's life, he hated his father, who admonished him not to "stay in the States, where you have to live like a nigger with niggers" (62).

The third real confession Hughes makes is about the deep pain of losing his relationship with his patron, Mrs. Charlotte Osgood Mason, the rich, elderly White woman he called "Godmother." When she ends her patronage of and friendship with Hughes, the anger he feels makes him physically ill even a decade later in retelling the incident. This may not be something students can relate to, but it helps them to better understand Hughes the man.

In *The Big Sea*, Hughes embeds other people's stories into his own story, a device not typical of autobiography. While his publishers at Knopf had allowed Hughes free rein in his poetry and short stories, they did not believe there was an audience for the stories about Black folk in his autobiography. Who would want to read about these folks, they asked, or about the artists, performers, and writers of the Harlem Renaissance? It took determination and courage on Hughes's part and the support of White critic and mentor Carl Van Vechten to convince publishers to publish the work as Hughes wanted it, making him truly earn the self-acclaimed title "the folk poet."

The Political Climate

Although Hughes may not have revealed deep secrets about his own life, he did an excellent job of re-creating on the page the period in which he lived. He writes about the history of the wider world, his fascination with socialism, his interrogation before the McCarthy commission, and who the presidents of the United States were during his politically aware years. When he pulls up his nets and examines the fish inside, he determines which of them are significant to his life story—especially the influences on his writing—and which ones are not.

Hughes's politics can be an occasion for classroom debate. We know that Hughes made no secret of his politics, with the exception of denying membership in the Communist Party. The world knew of his radical leftist leanings. Students can research the McCarthy era and offer their own conclusions on the differences (or, if they wish, similarities) between the political climate of Hughes's times and that of today.

Creative Nonfiction

The Big Sea can be read as creative nonfiction as well as autobiography because though the base storyline is true, the actual accounts have been artistically created. Hughes in his wisdom tells enough about his life to make a wonderful story and suppresses those things that would have been painful to tell. Even so, occasionally a rawness appears in his writing, as in the statement about his parents, especially his mother, abandoning him to his grandmother and relatives "who were really no relation" (36). For Hughes, his autobiography was much more than a recounting of his life experiences: it included writing about the folk; it was a means of paying tribute to all the Black people who had shared their lives, directly or indirectly, with him.

Creative nonfiction is an increasingly significant genre for writing teachers. You can create written assignments using sections of *The Big Sea* as a model. Ask students to do two pieces of writing: First they write a two-page factual account of a particular event or experience in their lives. Then they rewrite the piece as creative nonfiction. Ask students to describe how they made some of their choices as they included personal details and selected and reshaped the piece to make it more literary.

Through their exploration of this autobiography, students discover that literature becomes the metaphoric "Big Sea" for Hughes, and literature for the most part is what he gives us in *The Big Sea*. Hughes lets down his nets and he pulls. He ends *The Big Sea* by telling us that literature is what sustained him:

> Shortly poetry became bread; prose, shelter and raiment. Words turned into songs, plays, scenarios, articles and stories.
> Literature is a big sea full of many fish. I let down my nets and pulled.
> I'm still pulling.

Hughes gives us a wealth of information that our students can latch onto as they see elements of their own lives in his. He also provides insight into a life very different from their own.

IN THE CLASSROOM:
Langston's Life and Mine

Rather than rehash or summarize Hughes's life story, use *The Big Sea* as an opportunity to complicate the notion of what a life story is for those students who think that most autobiographies are written by old, famous people who have done something outstanding in their lives and want the world to know how they got to that point. Such "stories" are simply recitations of history for our students. To make autobiography more relevant and current for them, I reinforce the idea that Hughes was in his early thirties when he wrote *The Big Sea* but that he had been under pressure to write it from the time he was in his early twenties.

The sense of movement, instability, and migration that permeates Hughes's work also strikes a chord in many of my students, especially those who have had to move, for a myriad of reasons. Two things happen in studying Hughes's autobiography and writing an essay about their research. First of all, Hughes becomes a real person to the students. They no longer see him as a "character" in a novel but as a real person telling a real story. They are, then, separating autobiography from fiction. The other thing that happens is that they draw connections between the literature and their own lives. Sharise Robinson writes about Langston's journey in the following poem:

Langston's Journey

The trip home seemed so hard to swallow
Nowhere to rest, no one to follow
Sadness and anxiety cloud the time
time so priceless, time to unwind
Who better to understand you but your parents
Words not forgotten, but hardly spoken
To change a name would amount to nothing but a heathen
Understand is all I ask
Understand how hard I try
To measure up to you and I
To conform to the society where white is high class
But where I am is just a thing of the past
No one will listen, no one dear brother
To a nigger too good to stay in his place
Ahead of my time, ahead of my race
But you I will never escape
Part of me is lost, the other was stolen
To say I would amount to nothing golden.

Other students use this opportunity to write about their own travels. Dorian Donald, who migrated to Kansas from Arkansas, had strong personal reactions to the stories in *The Big Sea*. His memories are just as poignant as Hughes's.

I thought if I moved to Kansas it would be different. Wrong! In Arkansas, we as blacks knew how Caucasians felt about us. In Kansas they give us illusions and their true colors always shine. My dad would give advice on how to deal with ignorance or racism by telling me that I'm American I have the rights as every one else. I have had several racial slurs and comments by people I thought were my friends. The advice I would give them is tell me up front and don't put up a mirage that you're my friend and call me nigger behind my back.

Betsy Timm, a young White girl, also wrote of her experiences in moving from place to place:

> While I have no idea how African Americans feel because of their mistreatment, I do have empathy for them because of situations that I have dealt with in my life. I know how it feels to be picked on for no other reason than you are not like everyone else. It all started when I moved to Montana the summer after my sophomore year. Naturally I was not looking forward to the move because I would have to switch schools and move twelve hundred miles away from my friends. But I really had no choice, so I packed up my things and looked forward to living in the mountains and enjoying some skiing.

Crystal Ashton responded with a poem based on the young Hughes's long nights alone. She connected his experiences to the image of snakes in the biblical Adam and Eve story, approaching Hughes's conduct from a strictly Old Testament position. The young Langston, she believes, cast himself out of Eden the night he cried in shame about his conversion.

> What's the difference with this one,
> that no one'll come a run,
> His eyes are dark brown and his hair is the same,
> but he sleeps in a bed full of snakes and shame.
> Now when these snakes attack,
> Ohhh they hold on real tight,
> And you couldn't break loose with all of your might.
> The black ones just stare, it's the white ones you fear,
> But the child just lays there, and sheds but one tear.
>
> The tear is not for terror for this boy is brave,
> Its for the long nights ahead, in this hell-hole grave.

Regardless of the religious viewpoint here, what is significant is the intensity of the student's involvement with Hughes's experience. The situations Hughes writes about are most often very different from students' own lives, but students find a connection and relevance.

As mentioned earlier, the students can write autobiographical passages, using Hughes's work as a model, revealing as little or as much about their lives as they wish. I prefer to launch them into biography. This provides an opportunity for them to learn about some of the famous people to whom they haven't been exposed, but they could write about the "regular" people in their lives as well. Biography gives them more emotional distance than does writing about themselves.

Two exercises work particularly well for biography. In the first, I have students choose an individual to focus on; this person doesn't necessarily have to be a parent, but it does have to be someone to whom they have access. In fact, I strongly recommend that this person be someone they will have access to more than once. They can choose a friend, neighbor, relative, or even classmate. Their job in this assignment is to be the recorder of someone else's life. After they interview their subject, they write a biography of that person and share it with their subject. The interviewee can then approve or disapprove of the information in the biography. Then the student writes the final version.

In the second assignment, which is more of a library assignment, I have students choose someone who has had a significant impact, for better or worse, on a culture. I define culture as "shared experiences," which literally opens wide the exercise. My caveat to them in this exercise is that they must choose someone they know other people have written about. Since they won't be able to have conversations with Hitler or Mother Theresa, they have to rely on their subjects' biographies and autobiographies and what other people have said about them.

Some of the students have impressed me by personally contacting some of their subjects directly. They have written to places such as the Tiger Woods Foundation and the James Dobson Focus on the Family organization for more information and used the information they received in their biographies.

In both assignments, the final report has to have a cover with a picture of the subject on it, an original title, the student's name, and, for historical purposes, my name and the course title and semester. The report also has to have a back cover and be bound in some manner so that it makes a book. Students have been so proud of their projects that they have asked me not to mark in their books. They have requested everything from simply telling them what their grade is to using tabs to mark their errors. One student even included paper for me to make my comments on. They all have a genuine sense of accomplishment and pride in their work when they see their biography as a book with their name on the cover.

7 Keep It Simple, Sweetheart: The Jesse B. Semple Stories

■ ■

When Langston Hughes accepted a seat and a beer from a young Harlemite in a bar one night, he had no idea that the most famous character in Black literature, Jesse B. Semple, would evolve from the conversation. Hughes's stories about this character first appeared in a newspaper column of the *Chicago Defender*. Later they were collected and published as books. Donna Akiba Sullivan Harper, in her book *Not So Simple*, argues that the illusion of simplicity that typifies Langston Hughes's work is best exemplified by Jesse B. Semple. As Sullivan suggests, the character of Semple may have emerged from a highly comic conversation about vehicle cranks with a neighbor in Harlem, but Hughes's messages run deeper than they appear on first reading. The real-life individual, through the fictional character Semple, represents the cultural, social, economic, and history-making lives of most African Americans, especially northern migrants, during the era between the World Wars. Since the collections are long, you can assign students one story each for an in-class discussion. In analyzing the stories, students can construct a history of the period.

Many of the messages Hughes gave us through Semple are still appropriate, and students can learn much from Hughes's respect for all people. Langston Hughes was the kind of person who my grandmother would say never met a stranger. He loved

Harlem and he loved the people of Harlem. Each person Hughes met had a life that he saw as valuable. He also saw them as worthy subjects of his writing. You can use these stories as tools for teaching folklore—that is, the stories of the folk—and also for teaching how culture can be captured, preserved, and shared.

In discussing folklore, invite students to bring in the folklore that is part of their culture for a mutual exchange. This opens their eyes to the common threads in their cultures as well as the interesting, sometimes quaint, but always thought-provoking and enriching differences between individual families and groups.

The Main Characters

The Simple stories (so-called because Hughes subtitled the tales "Just be simple," and because he vacillates between calling the character "Semple" and "my simple-minded friend," which he shortens to "Simple") are a composite of people, mostly transplanted southerners, whom Hughes knew and others he had only heard about in Harlem. They remember vividly their lives in the South, which were filled with racism and denigration, and compare the South to the newness of Harlem. The liberty they feel having left the confines of the South is celebrated in these stories.

The character of Simple offers teachers an opportunity to draw students into the text. As previously mentioned, the inspiration for these stories was a neighbor of Hughes's in Harlem. Langston tells the story of running into this man in a neighborhood bar, one of his favorite spots, and then of visiting barbershops where he begins to gather material for story ideas. Seizing every opportunity to learn more about the man, Hughes put together an endearing picture of his new friend. When his friend talks about his job in a war plant, Hughes asks what he makes. The rest of the story, which sounds like a forerunner to a Laurel and Hardy or an Eddie Murphy and Martin Lawrence sketch, led to the creation of Hughes's simpleminded friend.

> I said, "What do you make?"
> He said, "Cranks."
> I said, "What kind of cranks?"
> He said, "Oh, man, I don't know what kind of cranks."
> I said, "Well, do they crank cars, tanks, buses, planes or what?"
> He said, "I don't know what them cranks crank."
> Whereupon his girlfriend, a little put out at this ignorance of his job, said, "You've been working there long enough. Looks like now you ought to know what them cranks crank."
> "Aw, woman," he said, "you know white folks don't tell colored folks what cranks crank." (Hughes, *Best of Simple*, vii, viii)

This man and his girlfriend were long lost to Hughes by the time these stories started to appear in print, but like the other "genial souls" in Harlem who freely talked about their lives, their loves, their disappointments, their joys, and their government, they live still in the Simple stories.

At this point, you can introduce your students to the literary concept of Everyman because that is precisely what Hughes is creating through this character—a Black Everyman. Let students suggest how Simple fills that role in African American culture. Jesse B. Semple was, according to literary critics James A. Emanuel and Theodore L. Gross, the one great fictional character that Hughes was to conceive (195). Encourage students to consider why scholars and critics have elevated Simple to the position of the most famous character in Black fiction. Does Simple deserve all this praise? How does he represent the average Black working man in the United States in the 1940s? What does the play on the original name (Jesse B. Semple) suggest about Hughes's treatment of this character?

To balance the Simple character, Hughes creates another character as a foil, an educated narrator with whom Simple converses, one who Hughes admits was really himself in the beginning, though he later names him "Boyd." This is an opportunity for teachers to talk about how character functions as an element of fiction. A writing assignment in comparing and contrasting the characters will be effective in helping students identify the extent to which both characters become more (or less) meaningful when set off against each other. In this case, Simple is a transplanted southerner who is hardworking, honest, basically moral, inquisitive, opinionated, loving and a lover, not particularly well educated, and candid with his mostly uninformed but pointed thoughts. The bar represents for him an important part of his life. Boyd, by contrast, is in the bar "observing life for literary purposes" (*Best of Simple* 12). He represents an educated inquisitor who learns of the thoughts, feelings, and desires of the common folk. He is college educated, sophisticated, worldly, and insightful. Although they appear to be representative of opposite ends of the African American spectrum, these characters are deeply similar. Let students uncover the similarities and differences. As they learn about these men, both Black and proud of it in a society that does not value Blackness, and both participating in the rich life of Harlem, the Mecca of Negro society, students also learn about Harlem in the 1940s.

"Folks is friendly in Harlem," Simple declares, a fact that makes him feel like he has the "world in a jug and the stopper in [his] hands" (*Best of Simple* 21). Harlem represents a rich, vibrant Black world operating fully within a larger White world. Simple gives us that Black world, a world that has enriched not only Black but also American history, a world that can come alive and engage your students.

Simple and Boyd's stories have withstood the test of time because readers share those experiences with them. They see their lives in the context of the larger world and their place within that world.

Names and Naming Traditions

The Simple stories can also help students of all ethnic groups learn about African American traditions. One of particular interest is the naming ritual.

Slaves often named their children after relatives so that if they were separated, which they often were, they would be able to find one another when they were freed or had escaped. Simple's story of his name is a humorous look at that tradition. Named after his dark-skinned, hard-drinking grandfather named Jess, Simple confesses that his real name is Jess Semple. As they read further about how Simple's name evolved on the playground to "Simple Simon," students can become more sensitive to their own names, the nicknames children use, and the wider implications of ethnic identity: name changes that a "melting pot" society requires, immigration officers who changed names they couldn't spell, the teasing children experience because of their names, and, today, pride in unique names that create identity.

African American Women in Harlem

Hughes doesn't stop with simply telling the stories of Black men through Jesse B. Semple; the stories are also filled with the lives of African American women in Harlem. You can approach the stories, then, from a gendered perspective. Ask your students about the women characters that Hughes creates. Can students make any generalizations about his attitude toward women? What's missing? What's highlighted in these portrayals? In the Simple stories, we meet Simple's wife, Isabel, whom he hasn't divorced but lives estranged from; the society woman Sadie Maxwell-Reeves; Joyce, "the woman he loves today" (*Best of Simple* viii), who encourages his jealousy as an expression of his love; the party-girl Zarita, with her head "looking like a hurrah's nest" (24); Aunt Lucy, who was so Christian that she wouldn't even whip "nobody on a Sunday," but when Simple gave one of her best laying hens to a girl who didn't even go to their church, she made an exception and woke up one Sunday morning with a switch in her hand (75). Ask your students to identify these and others and to find some phrases from the text that capture the essence of these women.

Hughes allows that it would be "impossible to live in Harlem and not know at least a hundred Simples, fifty Joyces, twenty-five Zaritas, a number of Boyds, and several Cousin Minnies—or reasonable facsimiles thereof" (*Best* vii). These are the people whose lives were interrupted and then restarted when they moved from the problems of the South to a new life in the North. The North offered industry, a steady paycheck, hard work, cold winters, and loneliness. It also offered shared experiences in which, as nineteenth-century social activist Anna Julia Cooper argues, "like attracts like" (719). They moved into neighborhoods with people like themselves: hard-loving, hard-fighting, hardworking people. People who, "as long as Georgia is Georgia," plan to stay in the North.

The Sociopolitical Climate

The Simple stories also provide an opportunity to teach short lessons on the sociopolitical climate of the time. Students get to look at the Second World War from a Black perspective. In many ways, the 1940s were defined by World War II, the battle to conquer the advocates of Aryan superiority. President Franklin D. Roosevelt had announced the goals of the war as the Four Freedoms: freedom of speech, freedom of worship, freedom from want, and freedom from fear. This event is important to these stories in very specific ways. In his conversations with Boyd, Simple voices the ordinary Black person's thoughts and concerns about the war and home front conditions, as well as the government's role in granting those four freedoms to them. This historical background offers an opportunity to talk about the irony of segregated troops fighting to free Europe from racism. In the conversation between Simple and Boyd in "Simple on Military Integration," Hughes makes a powerful statement that is comparable to the legal argument that was the basis of the *Brown v. Board of Education of Topeka, Kansas*, case. Simple makes the case that just talking to resolve and end Jim Crow laws isn't getting it done, that getting "shot down is bad for the body . . . but to be Jim Crowed is worse for the spirit" (*Best of Simple* 81). Integrating the military to the point that Black officers were in charge of White troops was not to happen until many years later. Encourage your students to research this issue. Can they point to evidence of Jim Crow laws—stated or unstated—in today's society?

Teaching about war offers opportunities to ask critical questions about the justifications for war. In the Simple stories, the war industry provides the jobs, like the crank making that Hughes hears about that night in the bar in Harlem. Many Blacks, whose stories Hughes portrays in these tales, moved to the North so they could work in the plants.

You can find other sociopolitical issues that allow students to ask not just "what" but also "why" and "how" questions that can lead to cross-disciplinary projects. Ask students, for example, to evaluate how much or how little working and social conditions have improved since the time of the stories.

Hughes touches on the social strife between the migrants and the European immigrants who have come for the same purpose—jobs. How different is the situation today? How do free trade agreements and outsourcing have an impact on jobs for African Americans in the twenty-first century? Ask students in this context to read Simple's poem as he laments the status of Blacks who live under Jim Crow (forced segregation) in the South while migrants ("Greeks, Germans, Jews, / Italians, Mexicans / And everybody" [*Best of Simple* 30] but Simple) were readily integrated into society. Ask students to pick one issue today that Hughes would respond to in the way he responded to social issues in his own time and to describe the position he would take on it.

Other social conditions can help you frame questions for students' inquiry into the notion of peace and how Hughes complicates it. The end of war, for example, disrupts African Americans' lives by ending their employment and taking away their means of livelihood. Simple, in his pledge to help God make the world a better place, wonders what he can do, since the people in charge of the world seem determined to "run it into the ground in spite of all, throwing people out of work and then saying, 'Peace, it's wonderful!' Peace ain't wonderful when folks ain't got no job" (*Best of Simple* 7). Ask your students to unpack the irony of these words.

The cohesive community building that Hughes writes about in these stories can also be read as a criticism of them. Encourage students to make arguments for or against the critique that the stories are divisive and encourage separatism because Simple and Boyd and the other Harlemites function in the midst of a Black-only world.

The more deeply students explore the stories, the more likely they are to recognize that Hughes argues for a universality that transcends geographic and ethnic boundaries. He uses Simple's race and his ordinariness as a means to expand his composite character into a symbol of universal humanity. Simple is like the folk in our neighborhoods who are good-hearted, dignified, compassionate, funny, and straightforward. The Simple tales inspired and told the stories of the day-to-day triumphs and survivals of the average person. In fact, Hughes's use of Simple transcends race. Simple describes himself as "no dangerous man. I am what folks calls an ordinary citizen. Me, I work, pay my rent, and taxes and try to get along" (*Return of Simple* 75). Ask students to find and describe a Jesse Simple in their lives.

How the Stories Came to Be

When reading well-crafted fiction, we are so absorbed by story, so engaged with the action, so taken with the characters that we often forget that these have been constructed by a writer. Students will be interested to learn how Hughes put together this collection of stories and to know that the character evolved and developed over a period of time.

Simple first appeared February 13, 1943, in a weekly column Hughes wrote for the *Chicago Defender*, the third most widely read newspaper in African American communities in the 1940s and the most widely read of the five Black newspapers in Chicago. Originally writing nonfiction editorials for a column he called "Here to Yonder" (started in November 1942), Hughes after three months began the Simple stories.

It became Hughes's pattern to write a sometimes controversial or provocative editorial one week and then have Simple discuss the issue the next. Simple, as the voice of the largely not well-educated masses, represented the Here, and the Hughes persona, the voice of the well read and educated, represented the Yonder. Even though the topics often dealt with sensitive issues, Hughes, in his traditional writing style, used humor and the rhythm of the blues to make logical points.

His success in creating a well-loved character is a testament to Hughes's ability as a writer. Getting Simple off the editorial page and into book form, however, wasn't a simple matter. Hughes was forced to select the stories he considered to be best, omit others, and write more, polishing and refining his prose to meet the editorial standards of the publisher. These revisions to Simple expanded the audience beyond the African American readership of the Black press and even the largely White readership of the *New York Post*. In reading of the evolution of the stories, students learn that even for a great author, writing is an ongoing process. The revisions enabled Hughes to bring the earthy, obvious, honest portrayals of life in the United States to a wide audience.

IN THE CLASSROOM:
Just Be Simple

In creating the two characters Simple and Boyd, Hughes gave us a remarkable teaching tool. The characters are complex in thought, action, and attitude, yet they seem to present a simple binary. Helping students to recognize that there is no either/or in the two characters' conversations opens doors to their understanding of the subtleties of argument. In addition, the stories are simply a lot of fun. Students get involved through the humor and the comedic responses before they realize that they have learned something.

There are many, many Simple stories. Students can choose their favorites, and as long as they all have the same favorites, they can discuss the issues in the stories, how Hughes makes his points, and the roles that humor and music play.

Students can also stage discussions between their own Simple and Boyd and have them discuss current issues in the same manner used in the stories. Recent history provides many significant issues for discussion. Homeland security is a hot button right now; the government's implementation of extraordinary security measures is of enormous interest to students. Information on all sorts of topics is easily accessible, and everybody seems to have an opinion on every issue. It is important for students to appreciate the inner beauty of Simple's character. He is not stupid, and although students can portray him humorously as Hughes did in the stories, you need to encourage them to explore his character so that they see him not as a buffoon but as a lovable human being. Character analysis of Boyd can also work well as a classroom activity. He is the kind of character that has been described as never entering a room without speaking to someone. Again, a comparison-contrast essay would be a good activity in this context. Students can also create Simple-like and Boyd-like characters whom they name and develop themselves. Approaching these assignments with a lighthearted tone allows students to have fun, yet they must ground their arguments in good support.

8 Whose Way? Their Way! *The Ways of White Folks*

■ ■

As classroom teachers with limited amounts of time to devote to each assignment, we have to rely on concentrated lessons to provide rich insights into Hughes's work. I would love to teach full texts like *The Big Sea*, but time for the most part won't allow it, at least not without sacrificing something equally important. I also don't want my students to do a superficial reading of a work, which can sometimes happen when they're faced with reading a long book. Getting involved with the plot is one way for students to know the text, but teachers know that there are deeper ways for students to engage with literature, ways that will open up to them the messages, history, and culture embedded in the text.

Our focus is on training our students to read carefully and critically. Hughes's collection of short stories *The Ways of White Folks*, first published in 1934, is a rich assortment of stories, some previously published and some not, about the interrelationships between Black and White people in the United States. These stories are not simply about the Black-White binary in the 1930s. Their complexity forces students to think critically about many issues concerning and that concerned all of the United States during that time.

The stories are for the most part pessimistic about race relations in the United States because Hughes had spent a year (1932–1933) in the Soviet Union and was in his most politically radical left-wing phase. He spent the next year in Carmel, California, where he wrote and collected the stories for this book.

Assign your students some background reading on the political history of the time, at least on the relations between the Soviet Union and the United States and the ideologies of each country. Then, when reading the stories, students can discuss whether the cynicism is at times heavy-handed or depressing and how it is balanced by the way Hughes uses music in the stories. You'll need to guide your students to help them see how Hughes incorporates a blues narrative or a syncopated alternation between characters' highs and lows, their joys and their sadness. Note, for example, Hughes's use of music in "Poor Little Black Fellow" to emphasize the rift between Arnie and his White foster parents. Arnie voices his hatred of racism and segregation in the United States, confessing that he wants to stay in Europe and marry a White girl. Arnie's foster father considers him a "Nigger" (*Ways of White Folks* 154), which causes the permanent break between them. At that point in the story, the piano being played next door is louder than ever, music and dancing fill the air, and the lights form a golden necklace over the Champs-Elysées. Here, the music suggests the freedom implicit in Arnie's separation from his foster parents.

In the following guide, we look at four of the fourteen stories in the collection. You should, of course, read all fourteen yourself and make your own choices.

"Cora Unashamed"

Hughes is a master of the blues tale. A blues tale follows the beat of blues melodies, which start with pain or loss but end in triumph in a call and response pattern. The difference between text and music is that instead of the audience responding to the blues singer, the narrator plays both parts—both singer and audience. Hughes sets up the negative element of the story and then takes the protagonist to victory.

The first story in the collection, "Cora Unashamed," is a blues tale that begins with a description of Melton, Iowa, as "one of those miserable in-between little places" (*Ways* 3). In describing Melton, Hughes immediately alerts the reader to the sorrow that is to come: this is not a happy song of someone's life being played out. Cora is identified as one of the least important citizens of Melton. She is a "negress" in polite circles and a "nigger" in not-so-polite terms, sometimes with the noun "wench" added "for no good reason" (3). This description is particularly hard for students to accept, especially since the forty-year-old Cora evokes their sympathy; she is never offensive, except that "she sometimes cussed" (3). She has accepted being treated like a dog by her employers, the Studevants.

You can anticipate that your students will be uncomfortable with Cora's submissiveness, which is so much a part of the openly racist culture in which Cora lives. Help students recognize the circumstances that have made Cora so submissive. Is this job a way out of abject poverty for her? Can they argue that this job is the best choice among evils for her? Ask them to imagine the choices open to a poor Black woman of that generation. Are there present-day parallels? Such an activity will open their eyes to sociocultural issues of race, gender, and class.

Cora's love life, along with its limitations, is bound to be of interest to young students. Cora's choices have been limited by life: early on she had a transient "colored lover," the only man she remembers really wanting. There is a dearth of Black men in her world. Driven by loneliness, Cora's later relationship with a White immigrant laborer results in pregnancy. My students are almost completely unfamiliar with the attitude that this would be a source of shame. In contemporary times, having a baby outside of marriage is commonplace, and fewer people think badly of the women who do.

This is the moment to introduce the concept of irony—the contrast between the shame that society imposes on Cora and her own refusal to be ashamed. When her child, "a living bridge between two worlds" (7), is born, Cora is happy. And when her child dies, the normally humble Cora unleashes all her emotions and curses God.

As students read of Cora's suffering, they see her transfer her maternal love to her employers' mentally challenged daughter, Jessie, who becomes the daughter of Cora's heart. When Jessie grows up, she too has a relationship and becomes pregnant, which costs her her own life. At this point, Hughes hammers home the idea that Cora's being "unashamed" of her relationship with a White boy, of her mulatto daughter, and of Jessie's pregnancy are the right responses to life experiences. Let students identify the many different actions and responses that help define the "ways of white folks" in contrast to Cora's. Hughes is heavy-handed when he makes his final point about shame and who should bear it.

Should you teach this story as a women's rights or anti-abortion piece? Since abortion is a highly charged and sensitive topic, it's best to focus on the other, related issues. My experience has been that students quickly latch onto that aspect of the story and ignore the theme. It's probably best to steer students away from the destructive forces of shame and embarrassment and toward a discussion of the positive forces of love and responsibility. Shifting the focus to relationships and the functional roles people play in those relationships avoids the polarization and moralizing that comes with abortion discussions. This story is much richer than one volatile issue. Ultimately, this is the story of powerful love, love so powerful that on the death of her child, Cora is not afraid to curse God. Students might flinch at such an outburst, but they recognize that Cora is a moral person, someone who can truly love and be unashamed to show her emotions on the death of both her "daughters."

In this era of welfare rights and reform, students often don't understand Cora's situation, in which she has few choices because of her economic conditions. You can ask them to research the history of these rights and return to Cora's plight in light of their findings. This allows them to see how Cora's economic conditions also affect her social choices, leading to isolation and loneliness because she has no people of her own race around to widen her options. My international students quickly identify with this point. Many of them are on the other side of the world from their families.

This story brings home the debate about race. Although most cultural critics argue that race is socially constructed and not biologically mandated, "Cora Unashamed" highlights the point made by Amy Gutmann in her book-length debate with K. Anthony Appiah about the truth of this theory; I agree with Gutmann that as long as we live in a country that defines itself racially, race is real (Appiah and Gutmann). Race certainly frames and informs Cora's life.

If time and circumstances allow, watch the PBS video of "Cora Unashamed" (Masterpiece Theatre's American Collection, 2001) and ask students to compare the film version with Hughes's original story.

"The Blues I'm Playing"

This is another story that weaves together the themes of music and race. Oceola Jones in "The Blues I'm Playing" breaks into a blues song on her piano as she frees herself from the bonds of White patronage, and "made the bass notes throb like tom-toms, the trebles cry like flutes, so deep in the earth and so high in the sky that they understood everything" (110). Students will discover that often for African American artists of this era, the way out of poverty and obscurity was through the patronage of an influential White person. Oceola's life paralleled Hughes's own life. Both Oceola and Hughes were artists who needed someone to support them so they could overcome racial and economic barriers. Hughes himself wrote under the patronage of Mrs. Rufus (Charlotte) Osgood Mason, whom he called "Godmother." Tyrannical in the extreme, Mrs. Mason dictated the form and content of the work of the artists she patronized.

Students can explore how Oceola Jones mirrors, albeit inversely, Hughes's experience as she finds herself shriveling inside from having to conform to fit her patron's desires. For Oceola, the classical music her patron is demanding she learn to play is not the music in her soul. When she finally makes the break from patronage and a paid-for life, she must live a life of poverty but her soul is freed. Released from its shackles of Whiteness, her spirit plays the music imbued in the tom toms of her people. By contrast, Hughes's patron, though generous in supporting Black artists, had her own skewed notions of Black culture and harassed Hughes to "be primitive, and know and feel the intuitions of the primitive" (*Big Sea* 325). When Hughes was forcibly released from his patronage by Mrs. Mason, he became physically ill, retreated to his mother's home in Cleveland, and could not write for a while.

Encourage students to evaluate this kind of patronage: How does it affect the recipient? Are the opportunities worth the risk? You could also broaden the discussion to patronage in other cultures and other times. (Shakespeare for example, depended on patronage.) Does patronage still exist? Can students offer modern-day examples?

"Home"

The third story we visit here also relies on a musical trope and also treats the issue of race. In "Home," the haunting melodies of the violin pervade the story of sensitive Black violinist Roy Williams, who is lynched for talking to a White woman. Williams returns home from traveling the world, with "bright stickers and tags" (32) in many foreign languages adorning his luggage, bringing his black violin case with him. Physically and emotionally sickened by the dissolute life he has experienced both in Europe and on his return to the United States, the well-dressed and good-looking Roy, who is dying, comes home to see his mother. Back in his hometown, for the first time in a long time he feels his color. He is an "uppity nigger" again (35).

Students can explore the music that surrounds Roy in Europe and in his hometown of Hopkinsville where he visits his mother. Is there a difference in the way Roy is received in Europe and in his hometown? How does the music reflect these differences? Encourage students to bring in to class different kinds of music that reflect the different moments in Roy's life.

The music in the story is interwoven with racial and cultural issues. Instead of the earthy jazz that Roy has been playing all over Europe, Roy's mother wants him to start playing for the Lord, since he "been playin' fo' de devil every night all over Europy" (37). Roy's subsequent concert of classical music, which evokes the appreciation of a White woman, Miss Reese, brings about his downfall.

Roy, who has forgotten the mores of the Deep South, is attacked and lynched for talking to Miss Reese and reaching out to shake her hand. The White folks leave his "brown body, stark naked, strung from a tree at the edge of town" (48). Hughes evokes the music of Roy's life by having his body hang like a violin for the wind to play. Ultimately, like all the stories in this collection, "Home" is a sad and bitter commentary on race relations.

"Father and Son"

This story also resonates with the sounds of haunting stringed melodies. "Father and Son" is the story of a "tall mulatto boy" (Bert) who takes his own life after murdering his White father. The relationship between the colonel and his mistress, "like so many between Negro women and white men in the South, began without love," but transformed into almost a "loving family," at least from Coralee's perspective. Coralee, who had been the colonel's mistress for thirty years, had "lived in the Big House, supervised his life, given him children, and loved him" (206). During his childhood, Bert, who looks White, mistakenly calls his father "papa" in front of guests and is brutally beaten by his father. As an adult, Bert returns from college to the plantation, determined to claim his birthright. The ensuing emotional battle between father and son, the racial overtones of their relationship, and the climactic ending are all topics that will engage your students. The story of Bert's need for his "papa," his father's brutal denial, the killing of the father, and ultimately Bert's suicide powerfully bring the story to a dramatic close.

Hughes then takes this story beyond the interracial relationship to focus on the deep-seated love of a mother for her child, much like the love we see expressed in Toni Morrison's *Beloved*. Rather than have her child tortured at the hands of a White mob, the boy's mother would rather see him dead. Indeed, she assists in his suicide. Hughes ends the story with the newspaper announcement that the colonel had no heirs. At least, no White heirs. The colonel has already acknowledged that he had five— four, with Bert gone—Black children. But they are invisible in White society.

My students are often troubled when at the end of the story Hughes shifts the focus from the love of a mother, who would hold back a desperate crowd so that her son can take his own life and not suffer the torture of the mob, back to "the ways of white folks," who as an angry mob are rushing to lynch him. Students often see the events as overkill. But in talking it out and exploring incidents of racial violence in their own times, they come to a better understanding of racism. Hughes infuses the sounds of the blues with the rapid, running rhythm of jazz as he tells the tragic story of the White father and his Black son, who had to die because the ways of White folk would not allow them to be family. The rhythm of the blues can be heard in the story of the confrontation between the colonel and Bert. The syncopated jazz rhythms can be heard in the dialogue between father and son, which culminates in the crescendo of Bert's "OK, but I'm not a nigger, Colonel Norwood, . . . I'm your son" (233).

IN THE CLASSROOM: Have It Your Way

The short stories in *The Ways of White Folks* offer students multiple ways to engage with literature precisely because they are short and because they are filled with action. After reading the stories, student Susan Thomas offered these comments:

> After hearing the facts from presentations and researching [Langston Hughes] myself, I feel that without writers like him the American readers would not know how African Americans lives were like and what they had to endure from others. His stories gave their lives voices and revealed the realities of what was really going on in America.

Student responses to these stories ran the spectrum from becoming very involved with the characters to dismissing them as too dramatic to be real. Chris Brown, in responding to Oceola Jones and her patron in "The Blues I'm Playing," values the friendship of Oceola and her patron above everything else:

> [I] felt almost saddened that the great relationship that the two women shared had finally come to an end. Oceola, and all that she had grown into, would now be on her own, once again forced to support herself. Mrs. Ellsworth, the lonely widow, would no longer have the company of her most prized and interesting protégé. The two women would no longer have the company of each other. I put down this story wondering how the two could be so close, yet still throw away a beautiful friendship in a moment of stubbornness. The two women had grown so much together.

Rachelle Kilgore said that if she "could have witnessed Oceola break out the blues for Mrs. Ellsworth at the end of the story," she would have given her "a standing ovation. I was glad that Oceola was not willing to give up her happiness for the sake of fame or artistry." Stephanie Darveaux can relate to this story because she "has a boyfriend who is black and sometimes [her] friends try to get him to act 'white.'" This same story made Mark Baker reflect on the differences between people:

> Some people do things that other people dream of doing, but those people have a different dream for their own lives and want another person's job. What makes one person happy doesn't mean it will make everyone happy. Oceola Jones's soul was in Harlem and at the end of the story it showed. This paper really inspired me to look at people in a new way and seriously try to figure out who they really are. Oceola Jones and Mrs. Ellsworth were like day and night, the only thing they had in common was they loved the piano.

Rachelle Kilgore read stories that were not included in the packet I handed out on *The Ways of White Folks* and responded to Hughes's short story "The Gun":

> For most of the story I found myself sympathizing with Flora Belle and the hard life she had to live moving from town to town. Flora Belle is a character that is so vulnerable and susceptible to external as well as internal forces. This fact that she is vulnerable makes her relatable to the audience. It is my belief that all of humanity is susceptible of these forces, and in that way Hughes is relating to his audience through Flora Belle.

It is wonderful when, like Rachelle, our students are so inspired by literature that they go above and beyond the reading assignment to explore on their own. Hughes provides a plethora of significant pieces for our students to discover.

Conclusion: We've Heard from You, Langston; Now We Can Do Something

Few writers have given teachers the opportunity to explore as many different genres with their students as has Langston Hughes. His life was a remarkable journey that readers can share through the emotional underpinnings of the work of this most gifted poet. His autobiography *The Big Sea* is filled with the music of a life that traveled many roads. His novel *Not without Laughter* crafts the lives of a family rich with longing and song. His short stories are filled with the euphony and cacophony of living Black in White America. But his poetry—ah, his poetry. The poetry of Langston Hughes carries music and a magic that fills our souls with the sounds and the rhythms of life—American life.

It can be a challenge to encourage our students to search for a deeper meaning and understanding, whether they are reading autobiography, novel, poetry, or short story. It is also challenging for us as teachers to keep from making an emotional investment in the reading and then forcing our views on our students. I have bitten my tongue more than once to keep from saying, "Well, when I read it, I think this is what he means." This is, after all, literature study, and literature has the power to draw us deeply into stories. Besides, my response to the work is not fixed. I get different meanings from some of the works each time I read them.

For me, the reward comes when students see that Cora's being unashamed to love a little White girl with intellectual challenges is just like their Aunt Jessie who took care of the foster care boy that nobody liked because he stole from them. My hard work seems like less of an effort as my students cheer Oceola when she gives up a cushy life living off somebody else's money in order to play the music that her soul craves, and then compare Oceola's life to their mother's black sheep of a brother, who got thrown out of the house because he wanted to be a rock musician instead of an architect. I guide my students to discovery; it is a joy when I watch them recognize the parallel between their parents' pushing them to follow in their footsteps or in their role model's footsteps and Hughes's father pushing him to go to school so that Langston can learn something that will allow him to make a good living. We have all been there at one time or another in our own lives. In my case, when I was growing up my mother, a nurse, kept hammering home that I should be a doctor so that I could live an economically comfortable and emotionally rewarding life. I knew she meant an MD, not a PhD. The point is that while we can't give our students those connections between the literature and their lives, we can guide them to find these connections for themselves. Our students come into our classrooms with their own set of experiences through which they will filter their reading. All of those experiences are different.

My goal is to have all my students eventually respond to the reading as Matt Schneider did:

> One thing I liked a lot about Hughes's poetry is the fact that he made me read critically. He makes the reader really search for the meaning of the poems. Although it is sometimes hard for me to find the literal meanings of poems, it keeps me very interested in what I am reading. I like a challenge and that is what he gave me in most of his poems.

My students have found various ways to interpret Hughes's work. What is wonderful is that each of them has been able to link these stories to his or her own life, giving it a deeper significance. These connections are not things we can hand to them or even point out to them as they read. We are pedagogues—our job description comes from the Greek word meaning "to guide." We can point the way, but the students have to embark on this journey of discovery on their own. Fortunately for us as teachers, the writing of Langston Hughes is so rich that our students can interpret his work in a myriad of ways, and each one will be right. They will laugh and sing and sigh as they discover the wonderful legacy of literature that Hughes has bequeathed to us all.

Chronology

1859   John Brown's raid on Harper's Ferry. Langston
        Hughes's grandmother's first husband, Sheridan
        Leary, died in the raid. She was later honored by
        President Teddy Roosevelt as the last surviving
        widow of the raid, an event that made a significant
        impact on young Langston.

1899   James Nathaniel Hughes and his wife, Carolina
        "Carrie" Langston Hughes, move to Joplin, Missouri,
        in search of greater racial and financial freedom,
        which they do not find.

1902   February 1: James Langston Hughes is born in
        Joplin, Missouri.

1903   October: James Nathaniel Hughes abandons Carrie
        and baby Langston and moves to Mexico.
        Carrie takes Langston to live with his grandmother,
        Mary Leary Langston in Lawrence, Kansas.

1907   Carrie Langston Hughes moves to Topeka, Kansas, in
        one of the short periods he lived with her. Langston
        attends first grade in Topeka. His mother takes him
        to the library, where he falls in love with books.

1908   Carrie, anticipating reconciliation with James, takes Langston to visit his father in Mexico. An earthquake scares her back to Kansas. His parents were never to reconcile.

1903–15 Hughes lives primarily with his grandmother in Lawrence, Kansas. He attends Pinckney School in Lawrence for second grade.

1909   The National Association for the Advancement of Colored People (NAACP) is founded.

1914   Carrie Hughes marries Homer Clark. Langston does not live with her and her new husband.

1915   April: Mary Langston, Hughes's grandmother, dies. Langston is left in the care of his grandmother's close friends "Auntie" and "Uncle" Reed in Lawrence. He lives with them for a while and then moves to Lincoln, Illinois, to live with his mother and begins the eighth grade there.

1918   Langston publishes short stories and poems in the *Central High Monthly Magazine* put out by his high school in Cleveland, Ohio. He excels in track and other sports.

1919   Langston spends the summer with his father in Mexico.

1920   Langston graduates from high school in Cleveland.

On a train to Mexico to visit his father again, Hughes writes "The Negro Speaks of Rivers" as he crosses the Mississippi River in St. Louis.

1921   Hughes attends Columbia University for one year. He drops out to work odd jobs. His father wanted him to be an engineer; Langston discovers he wants to be a writer.
Hughes discovers Harlem and meets many influential people, including Dr. W. E. B. DuBois, Countee Cullen, and Jessie Fauset, writer and literary editor of *The Crisis*.
"The Negro Speaks of Rivers" is published in *The Crisis*.
May 22: *Shuffle Along* by Noble Sissle and Eubie Blake is the first musical revue written and performed by African Americans. The play opened at Broadway's David Belasco Theater.

1922   Hughes withdraws from Columbia University. He continues to publish in *The Crisis*.
First anti-lynching legislation is approved by House of Representatives.
The Harmon Foundation is established to promote Black participation in the fine arts.

1923   Hughes writes "The Weary Blues" after visiting a Harlem cabaret. He travels to Africa and Europe while working on a merchant ship.
Writes "I, too."

Opportunity: A Journal of Negro Life is founded by the National Urban League; Charles S. Johnson is editor.
The Cotton Club opens in Harlem.
Several literary and political texts, including Jean Toomer's *Cane* and Marcus Garvey's *Philosophy and Opinion of Marcus Garvey*, are published.

1924   Hughes returns to Harlem.
March 21: Civic Club Dinner sponsored by *Opportunity* brings Black writers and White publishers together. This event is considered the formal launching of the New Negro Movement.

1925   Hughes moves to Washington, D.C.
"The Weary Blues" wins him first prize in the *Opportunity* contest. Other winners are Countee Cullen and Zora Neale Hurston.
Small's Paradise Nightclub opens in Harlem.

1926   Hughes moves back to Harlem. He publishes *The Weary Blues*, his first collection of poems.
Hughes enrolls in Lincoln University in Pennsylvania.
Hughes, Wallace Thurman, Zora Neale Hurston, Aaron Douglas, and Richard Bruce Nugent launch a literary magazine, *Fire!!!* Ironically, only one issue was published, due to lack of funding and a fire that burned the office to the ground.
Hughes publishes his seminal essay, "The Negro Artist and the Racial Mountain," in *Nation*.

1927   Charlotte Osgood Mason becomes a patron of many
New Negro artists, including Hughes and Hurston.
Hughes publishes *Fine Clothes to the Jew*.
In Abraham's Bosom, by Paul Green, with an all-Black
cast, wins the Pulitzer Prize.
Porgy by Dorothy and DuBose Heyward opens at the
Theater Guild on Broadway.
A'Lelia Walker, daughter of Madame C. J. Walker,
opens a tea room literary salon called "The Dark
Tower."

1929   Hughes graduates from Lincoln University.
The Negro Experimental Theater, Negro Art Theater,
and National Colored Players are founded.
Wallace Thurman's play *Harlem*, written with
William Jourdan Rapp, opens at the Apollo Theater
and becomes hugely successful.
October 29: Black Thursday; Stock Exchange
crashes.

1930   Hughes publishes *Not without Laughter*, his first novel.
The Green Pastures (musical), with an all-Black cast,
opens on Broadway.

1931   August 16: A'Lelia Walker dies.
Hughes publishes *Dear Lovely Death* and *The Negro
Mother, and Other Dramatic Recitations*.

1932   Hughes travels to the Soviet Union.
Publishes *The Dream Keeper* and *Scottsboro Limited*.

1934   Publishes *The Ways of White Folks*, his first collection
          of short stories.

1935   Awarded a Guggenheim Fellowship.
          March 19: Harlem Race Riot.
          October 10: *Porgy and Bess*, with an all-Black cast,
          opens on Broadway.
          October 25: Hughes's play *Mulatto,* the first full-
          length play by a Black writer, opens on Broadway.

1936   Hughes writes the play *Troubled Island*.

1937   Writes the play *Soul Gone Home*.
          Becomes a journalist for the *Baltimore Afro-American*
          and covers the Spanish-American War.

1938   Writes the play *Don't You Want to Be Free?*
          Founds the Harlem Suitcase Theater and a theater in
          Los Angeles.

1940   Publishes *The Big Sea*, the first of two autobiographies.
          Is awarded a Rosenwald Fellowship.

1942   Publishes *Shakespeare in Harlem*, a book of poems.

1943   Writes for the *Chicago Defender* and creates his
          Simple character in columns for the paper.
          Awarded an honorary LittD by Lincoln University.

1947   Poet-in-residence at Atlanta University.
          Publishes *Fields of Wonder*.

1949   Publishes *One Way Ticket*.

1950   Publishes *Simple Speaks His Mind*, his first volume of Simple sketches.

1951   Publishes a translation of Federico García Lorca's *Gypsy Ballads*.
        Publishes *Montage of a Dream Deferred*, his first book-length poem, in which he successfully sustains jazz cadences.

1952   Edits *The First Book of Negroes*, an anthology.

1953   Subpoenaed to appear before the House Un-American Activities Committee in Washington, D.C., Hughes is considered a security risk by the FBI until 1959.

1954–55 Publishes a number of books for young readers including *Famous American Negroes*.
        Publishes *The First Book of Jazz*.
        The Sweet Flypaper of Life, with Roy DeCarava, is published.

1956   Publishes *I Wonder as I Wander: An Autobiographical Journey*, his second autobiography.

1958   Publishes *The Langston Hughes Reader*.
        Coedits *The First Book of Negro Folklore*.
        Publishes *Tambourines to Glory*, a novel that was later (1963) to appear as a musical play.

1959	Publishes *Selected Poems of Langston Hughes*.
1960	Edits the anthology *An African Treasury: Articles, Essays, Stories, Poems by Black Africans*.
1961	Inducted into the National Institute of Arts and Letters. Publishes *Ask Your Mama*. Publishes *The Best of Simple*.
1962	Publishes *Fight for Freedom: The Story of the NAACP*.
1963	Publishes *Five Plays by Langston Hughes*. Edits the anthology *Poems from Black Africa*.
1964	Publishes *New Negro Poets: U. S. A.*
1965	Defends Martin Luther King, Jr., from attacks by militant Blacks.
1966	Appointed by President Lyndon B. Johnson to lead the U.S. delegation to the First World Festival of Negro Arts in Dakar, Senegal.
1967	Edits the anthology *The Best Short Stories by Negro Writers*. May 22: Dies of prostate cancer in New York City. *The Panther and the Lash: Poems of Our Times*, his last volume of poems, is published posthumously.

1969   The Langston Hughes Community Library and
        Cultural Center (Queens Borough Public Library),
        the first public institution named after the Poet
        Laureate of Black America, opens.

1973   *Good Morning Revolution: Uncollected Writings of Social
        Protest* is published.

1994   *The Collected Poems of Langston Hughes*, edited by
        Arnold Rampersad and David Roessel, is published.
        Five Plays by Langston Hughes is published.

Glossary

ALAMEDA: a public walkway or promenade usually bordered with trees

AUTOBIOGRAPHY: the telling in narrative form of one's own life story in which the writer has a "creative and imaginative engagement with the past" (Tidwell xvi).

BLUES: a unique Black folk musical form that emerged in the latter half of the nineteenth century; a narrative of lives that prompts the old adage, "to laugh to keep from crying." The blues usually end in triumph for the wronged person.

COLLAPSE TIME: to move freely from one time period to another; to bring a different era to the present

ESSENTIALISM: a theory that assumes that the ideas, actions, philosophies, morals, intellect, etc., of a group can be attributed to each individual in that group

FRAME: the controlling theme of the story. Sometimes presented as a story within a story, the story told in story time is the frame story.

FUNCTIONAL RELATIVES: people who function in a relational role that is not their "real" role. For example, an aunt raising a nephew is a functional mother.

HARLEM RENAISSANCE: the intellectual and artistic aspects of the New Negro Movement of the 1920s and 1930s

HARPER'S FERRY: the federal arsenal where John Brown and his group were captured in 1859, ending his battle against slavery

JAZZ: an improvised music of definable forms, such as call and response exchanges between the instruments

JIM CROW: legalized segregation. Became formalized with the *Plessy v. Ferguson* decision that made "separate but equal" the law of the land.

JOHN BROWN: self-proclaimed emissary of God to end slavery. He was hanged for his failed attack on Harper's Ferry.

MANN ACT: law restricting interstate transportation of people for illegal purposes. Enacted in response to Jack Johnson's physical abuse of White women.

McCARTHYISM: a mid-twentieth-century political attitude that opposed elements thought to be subversive to democracy, especially communism (named after Senator Joseph R. McCarthy)

MEMOIR: a narrative telling of one's personal life story in which the writer "points to the past as history and fact" (Tidwell xvi)

MULATTO: a biracial person, especially with one European American and one African American parent

NATIONAL ASSOCIATION FOR THE ADVANCEMENT OF COLORED PEOPLE (NAACP): an interracial organization developed from the Niagara Movement at the turn of the twentieth century to improve race relations and promote social equity in the United States

NEW NEGRO MOVEMENT: the political, social, and historical transformation of the lives of African American people in the 1920s and 1930s

ORAL LITERATURE: stories passed down orally from generation to generation that reflect the myths, legends, and heroes of a culture

PATRONAGE: providing financial support to an artist to allow him or her to develop his or her craft

PERIODIZATION: the time frame for a particular event, era, etc.

PROLETARIAT: the laboring socioeconomic class

RACIAL UPLIFT: the desire to elevate public opinion and conditions of a race

RACISM: the belief that the primary determinant of human traits and capabilities is race and that racial difference produces an inherent superiority of a particular race

SEGREGATION: social separation, especially by race

SEXISM: the belief that the primary determinant of human traits and capabilities is gender and that gender differences can cause one gender to be superior to another

SOCIAL EQUITY: when all people have the same rights and protection of the law and access to public accommodations

TROPE: a word or expression in literature that comes to symbolize something bigger than itself. For example, trains or train whistles are tropes for a character's desire to travel.

Selected Bibliography

This is not a complete bibliography of the works by and about Langston Hughes, who wrote prolifically and in many genres. The sources included here constitute some of the strongest of his works, but teachers interested in learning more about Hughes will find a plethora of additional sources.

Primary Works

HUGHES, LANGSTON. *The Best of Simple*. 1961. New York: Hill and Wang, 2000.

———. *The Big Sea: An Autobiography*. 1940. New York: Hill and Wang, 1963.

———. *The Block: Poems*. Illus. Romare Bearden. New York: Viking, 1995.

———. *The Book of Rhythms*. 1954. New York: Oxford UP, 1995.

———. *Carol of the Brown King: Nativity Poems*. New York: Athenaeum Books, 1998.

———. *Dear Lovely Death*. Amenia, NY: Troutback, 1931.

———. *Don't You Turn Back: Poems*. Sel. Lee Bennett Hopkins. New York: Knopf, 1969.

———. *The Dream Keeper and Other Poems*. 1932. New York: Knopf, 1996.

———. *Fields of Wonder*. New York: Knopf, 1947.

————. *Fight for Freedom: The Story of the NAACP*. New York: Norton, 1962.

————. *Fine Clothes to the Jew*. New York: Knopf, 1927.

————. *The First Book of Africa*. New York: Franklin Watts, 1960.

————. *The First Book of Jazz*. 1955. New York: Ecco, 1995.

————. *The First Book of Negroes*. New York: Franklin Watts, 1952.

————. *The First Book of Rhythms*. New York: Franklin Watts, 1954.

————. *The First Book of the West Indies*. New York: Franklin Watts, 1956.

————. *Freedom's Plow*. New York: Musette, 1943.

————. *I Wonder as I Wander: An Autobiographical Journey*. 1956. New York: Thunder's Mouth, 1986.

————. *Jazz*. New York: Franklin Watts, 1982.

————. *The Langston Hughes Reader*. 1958. New York: George Braziller, 1971.

————. *Laughing to Keep from Crying*. 1952. Mattituck, NY: Aeonian, 1976.

————. *Laughing to Keep from Crying and 25 Jesse Semple Stories*. Ltd. ed. Franklin Center, PA: Franklin Library, 1981.

————. *Montage of a Dream Deferred*. New York: Henry Holt, 1951.

————. *A New Song*. New York: International Workers Order, 1938.

————. *Not without Laughter*. 1930. New York: Collier, 1970.

————. *One-Way Ticket*. Illus. Jacob Lawrence. New York: Knopf, 1949.

————. *The Panther and the Lash: Poems of Our Times*. 1967. New York: Vintage Books, 1992.

————. *The Return of Simple*. Ed. Akiba Sullivan Harper. New York: Hill and Wang, 1994.

————. *Scottsboro Limited: Four Poems and a Play in Verse*. New York: Golden Stair, 1932.

———. *Selected Poems of Langston Hughes.* 1959. New York: Knopf, 1993.

———. *Shakespeare in Harlem.* New York: Knopf, 1942.

———. *Short Stories.* Ed. Akiba Sullivan Harper. New York: Hill and Wang, 1996.

———. *The Simple Omnibus.* Mattituck, NY: Aeonian, 1978.

———. *Simple Speaks His Mind.* 1950. Mattituck, NY: Aeonian, 1976.

———. *Simple Stakes a Claim.* New York: Rinehart, 1957.

———. *Simple's Uncle Sam.* New York: Hill and Wang, 1967.

———. *Simple Takes a Wife.* New York: Simon and Schuster, 1953.

———. *Something in Common, and Other Stories.* New York: Hill and Wang, 1963.

———. *The Sweet and Sour Animal Book.* New York: Oxford UP, 1994.

———. *Tambourines to Glory: A Novel.* New York: John Day, 1958.

———. *Thank You, M'am.* Mankato, MN: Creative Education, 1991.

———. *The Ways of White Folks.* 1934. New York: Vintage, 1971.

———. *The Weary Blues.* New York: Knopf, 1926.

Collaborations

BONTEMPS, ARNA, AND LANGSTON HUGHES. *The Pasteboard Bandit.* New York: Oxford UP, 1997.

———. *Popo and Fifina.* New York: Oxford UP, 1993.

DECARAVA, ROY, AND LANGSTON HUGHES. *The Sweet Flypaper of Life.* 1955. New York: Hill and Wang, 1967.

HUGHES, LANGSTON, AND ARNA BONTEMPS, EDS. *The Book of Negro Folklore.* New York: Dodd, Mead, 1958.

———. *The Poetry of the Negro, 1746–1970.* Garden City, NY: Doubleday, 1970.

HUGHES, LANGSTON, AND MILTON MELTZER. *African American History: Four Centuries of Black Life.* New York: Scholastic, 1990.

———. *Black Magic: A Pictorial History of the African-American in the Performing Arts.* New York: Da Capo, 1990.

HUGHES, LANGSTON, MILTON MELTZER, AND C. ERIC LINCOLN. *A Pictorial History of Blackamericans.* New York: Crown, 1983.

NICHOLS, CHARLES H., SEL. AND ED. *Arna Bontemps-Langston Hughes Letters, 1925–1967.* New York: Dodd, Mead, 1980.

Operas/Drama

HUGHES, LANGSTON. *Black Nativity.* Woodstock, IL: Dramatic Pub., 1992.

———. *The Negro Mother, and Other Dramatic Recitations.* 1931. Freeport, NY: Books for Libraries Press, 1971.

HUGHES, LANGSTON, AND ZORA NEALE HURSTON. *Mule Bone: A Comedy of Negro Life.* 1931. Ed. George Houston Bass and Henry Louis Gates, Jr. New York: HarperPerennial, 1991.

Secondary Works

ALLEN, JAMES. *Without Sanctuary: Lynching Photography in America.* Santa Fe, NM: Twin Palms, 2000.

APPIAH, K. ANTHONY, AND AMY GUTMANN. *Color Conscious: The Political Morality of Race.* Princeton, NJ: Princeton UP, 1996.

BERRY, S. L. *Langston Hughes.* Mankato, MN: Creative Education, 1994.

BONNER, PAT E. *Sassy Jazz and Slo' Draggin' Blues: Music in the Poetry of Langston Hughes.* New York: P. Lang, 1996.

CLIFTON, LUCILLE. "jasper texas 1998." *Discovering Arguments: An Introduction to Critical Thinking and Writing with Readings.* Ed. Dean Memering and William Palmer. Upper Saddle River, NJ: Prentice Hall, 2002.

COOPER, ANNA JULIA. "A Voice from the South." *The Heath Anthology of American Literature.* 3rd ed. Gen. Ed. Paul Lauter. Boston: Houghton Mifflin, 1998. 706–23.

Davis, Frank Marshall. *Livin' the Blues: Memoirs of a Black Journalist and Poet.* Ed. John Edgar Tidwell. Madison: U of Wisconsin Press, 1992.

Davis, Ossie. *Langston: A Play.* New York: Delacort, 1982.

DuBois, W. E. B. *The Souls of Black Folk.* 1903. New York: Knopf, 1993.

Duffy, Susan, ed. *The Political Plays of Langston Hughes.* Carbondale: Southern Illinois UP, 2000.

Early, Gerald, ed. *My Soul's High Song: The Collected Writings of Countee Cullen, Voice of the Harlem Renaissance.* New York: Doubleday, 1991.

Emanuel, James A., and Theodore L. Gross, eds. *Dark Symphony: Negro Literature in America.* New York: Free Press, 1968.

Gates, Henry Louis, Jr., and K. A. Appiah, eds. *Langston Hughes: Critical Perspectives Past and Present.* New York: Amistad, 1993.

Harper, Donna Akiba Sullivan. *Not So Simple: The "Simple" Stories by Langston Hughes.* Columbia: U of Missouri P, 1995.

Kirschke, Amy Helene. *Aaron Douglas: Art, Race, and the Harlem Renaissance.* Jackson: UP Mississippi, 1995.

Lewis, David Levering, ed. *The Portable Harlem Renaissance Reader.* New York: Viking, 1994.

―――. *When Harlem Was in Vogue.* New York: Knopf, 1981.

Locke, Alain LeRoy. *The New Negro: An Interpretation.* 1925. New York: Arno Press and *The New York Times,* 1968.

Rampersad, Arnold, ed. *The Collected Poems of Langston Hughes.* New York: Knopf, 1996.

―――. *The Life of Langston Hughes.* New York: Oxford UP, 1986.

Rampersad, Arnold, ed., and David Roessel, assoc. ed. *The Collected Poems of Langston Hughes.* New York: Vintage, 1995.

Tracy, Steven C. *Langston Hughes and the Blues.* Urbana: U of Illinois P, 1988.

Walker, Alice. *Langston Hughes, American Poet.* New York: Crowell, 1974.

———. *Langston Hughes, American Poet*. 1974. New York: HarperCollins, 2002.

Videotapes/Audiotapes

Cora Unashamed. Dir. Deborah M. Pratt. Masterpiece Theatre's American Collection. PBS Home Video, 2000.

The Harlem Renaissance and Beyond. Videorecording. Guidance Associates, 1990.

Langston Hughes: The Dream Keeper. Dir. St. Clair Bourne. South Carolina Educational Television Network, a New York Center for Visual History Production. Videorecording. Intellimation, 1988.

A Meditation on Langston Hughes (1902–1967) and the Harlem Renaissance: With the Poetry of Essex Hemphill and Bruce Nugent (1906–1987). Dir. Isaac Julien. Videorecording. SanKoFa Film and Video, 1992.

Internet Sites

Every effort has been made to provide current URLs and e-mail addresses, but because of the rapidly changing nature of the Web, some sites and addresses may no longer be accessible.

African-American Studies: Bibliography of Reference Books. Columbia University Libraries. 19 Jan. 2006 <http://www.columbia.edu/cu/libraries/subjects/afam/afambibl.html>.

Contemporary Authors Online. Detroit: Gale Research. <http://galenet.gale.com/m/mcp/db/ca/>.

Modern American Poetry. Ed. Cary Nelson. 19 Jan. 2006 <www.english.uiuc.edu/maps/>.

Schomburg Center Homepage. Schomburg Center for Research in Black Culture. New York Public Library. 19 Jan. 2006 <http://www.nypl.org/research/sc/sc.html>.

Author

Carmaletta M. Williams is professor of writing, literature, media communications, and African American studies at Johnson County Community College (JCCC) in Overland Park, Kansas. She has made numerous presentations and conducted workshops for middle and high schools, colleges and universities, and community groups, largely through the auspices of the Kansas Humanities Council. Williams earned Bachelor and Master of Arts degrees in English from the University of Missouri–Kansas City and a doctorate from the University of Kansas. She has won a number of distinguished teaching awards, including the Burlington Northern-Sante Fe Faculty Achievement Award, three Distinguished Service Awards from JCCC, the Carnegie Foundation for the Advancement of Teaching and Council for Advancement and Support of Education's Kansas Professor of the Year, and the League for Innovation's Innovation of the Year award for her videotape titled "Sankofa: My Journey Home," about her Fulbright-Hays Award study in Ghana, West Africa. Williams traveled to Guinea, West Africa, where as a guest of the government she established a faculty exchange between L'Ecole Nationale de Poste et Telecommunications and JCCC. She was an invited scholar to South Africa, where she interviewed citizens about their experiences during and after apartheid. Williams was awarded JCCC's first Diversity Award in September 2005.

This book was typeset by Electronic Imaging in Berkeley, Interstate, and Old Style 7.

The typefaces used on the cover include Trebuchet MS and Zurich Ex BT.

The book was printed on 50-lb. Williamsburg Offset paper by Versa Press, Inc.